Contents

For Monique and Cedric

Introductory Note

Musset's play tells the story of the assassination of the Duke of Florence by the young Lorenzo de Médicis. The fascination which the work exerts derives to a large extent from the enigmatic character of the main protagonist. From the outset Lorenzo engages our interest. Lucid, yet divided against himself, he stands apart from those characters who usually inhabit the world of French Romantic drama. As the action unfolds the complex and contradictory impulses which determine his behaviour are revealed. His motives are explored with great skill and subtlety. Lorenzo may appear to be pursuing clearly defined objectives but is he not driven by darker, more disturbing forces? To what extent is he consciously aware of the reasons which prompt him to act?

It would, however, be an error to define Musset's creation exclusively in terms of the portrayal of an individual life. *Lorenzaccio* is much more than that. It is an evocation, a splendid recreation of Florentine society in 1536. A broad tapestry unfolds before the reader's eyes as Renaissance Florence becomes a diverse, living reality. But if the setting is sixteenth-century Florence the preoccupations of the playwright are those of a Romantic and not a Renaissance dramatist. For if Musset remained in a number of respects faithful to his sources, he transformed his material by incorporating into his creation the sufferings of his own tormented soul and the temporal and social experience of nineteenth-century man living in a post-revolutionary world of change, instability and anxiety.

Lorenzaccio asks questions of fundamental importance concerning the meaning of history, the relationship between the individual and society and the possibility of transforming the social order through the practice of revolutionary violence. Are we dealing with a political play or with a work primarily interested in the moral problems of an individual? The question is legitimate but it misses the point. The two goals cannot be dissociated from one another. Lorenzo's predicament is grounded in the movement of history since his dilemma poses the problem of means and ends. The play teaches us that the problems of self are not isolated from the wider historical context: Lorenzo is searching for a new order capable at one and the same time of regenerating Florentine society and reunifying his own fragmented personality. We must take account of both the moral and the sociopolitical dimensions and attend to their interaction. To do otherwise is, in my view, to misconceive the true value of the text.

Musset was born in Paris in 1810. He came from an aristocratic family which showed distinct literary leanings and interests. Like his fellow poet Alfred de Vigny he was proud of his noble ancestry. Musset received his schooling in Paris at the Collège Henri IV. He was a successful pupil and carried off several prizes. By the late 1820s he seems to have made his mind up to leave his mark on French literature. He certainly was not deficient in ambition. In a letter of 1827 he wrote: 'je ne voudrais pas écrire, ou je voudrais être Shakespeare ou Schiller.'[1] The young writer was soon accepted by the literary world of Paris which recognised in Musset a new poet of talent and promise. In 1829 he published his *Contes d'Espagne et d'Italie* and this collection of verse, full of local colour and dramatic action as favoured by the fashion of the day, achieved a degree of success. Other poems and plays followed during the early years of the July Monarchy: *La Coupe et les lèvres*, *André del Sarto*, *Les Caprices de Marianne*, *Rolla*. *Lorenzaccio* appeared in August 1834 and was included in the second part of *Un Spectacle dans un fauteuil*. As the title suggests, Musset intended his work to be read rather than performed — he was still smarting from the total failure of his play *La Nuit vénitienne* which had been put on at the Odéon in December 1830.

The date of composition of *Lorenzaccio* has been a cause of considerable controversy. It was long held that the play had been written during the journey to Italy which Musset undertook in

[1] Musset, *Correspondance* (Paris, Mercure de France, 1907), 11.

December 1833 in the company of George Sand and which lasted until March 1834. It was somehow felt necessary for Musset to have visited Florence in order to make the city the setting for his play. Moreover, some remarks in Paul de Musset's biography of his brother lent support to this view. Jean Pommier, however, in an article of 1957 proved beyond doubt that *Lorenzaccio* had in fact been completed before December 1833. Pommier printed for the first time the text of a letter which Musset sent to François Buloz, the editor of the *Revue des deux mondes*, in January 1834. The letter clearly implies that Buloz had received the manuscript of *Lorenzaccio* before Musset left for Italy. This does not rule out the possibility that he revised his work after his return from Italy and prior to publication in August 1834. Critical opinion is nevertheless now agreed that for all intents and purposes *Lorenzaccio* was written in a period of intense creative activity between late June and early December 1833.

In other words the play was composed during the first months of Musset's celebrated love affair with the novelist George Sand. Indeed had it not been for the presence of George Sand it is unlikely that Musset would ever have tackled the subject at all. In 1833 Sand gave Musset a manuscript copy of her dramatic work, *Une Conspiration en 1537*. This had been written in 1831 and was probably intended for publication in the *Revue de Paris*. It remained, however, in manuscript form and did not appear in print until the twentieth century. Sand's text is a 'scène historique' which takes as its subject the murder of the Duke of Florence. It is quite short, comprising six scenes and running to some sixty-five pages in the edition by Paul Dimoff. *Une Conspiration en 1537* portrays Lorenzo's failure to fight a duel, his rehearsing the assassination with Scoronconcolo and other scenes with which the reader of *Lorenzaccio* is familiar. Musset's debt to Sand is beyond question; there are indeed some direct textual borrowings. *Lorenzaccio*, on the other hand, is a far more ambitous project. Musset went back to Sand's original source, Benedetto Varchi's *Storia Fiorentina*, in order to increase his historical perspective. He extended both the spatial and temporal dimensions. He endowed the characters with a life they lack in Sand's text. Above all, he brought to his play the power of his creative imagination. *Une Conspiration en 1537* is a relatively successful example of a minor genre; *Lorenzaccio* is a rich and complex masterpiece of Romantic art.

In the present study my intention is to introduce readers to one of the most fascinating literary texts of the nineteenth century. However, an acquaintance with French Classical tragedy often leaves the student somewhat ill-prepared for the encounter with Musset's vast array of characters and numerous changes of scene. In my view the best way for the new reader to approach *Lorenzaccio* is through an examination of the character of the main protagonist. For this reason my first chapter is devoted to this topic. There follows a discussion of the picture of social reality contained in the text. In Chapter 3 I relate the play to its historical context and indicate its relevance to the debate concerning the meaning of history which was current among Musset's contemporaries. Chapter 4 is given over to two specific matters: Musset's treatment of the theme of the mask and his attitude to the phenomenon of language. The final section looks at the question of dramatic coherence.

Note on the text

References throughout are to *Lorenzaccio*, ed. D.-P. and P. Cogny (Paris, Bordas, 1963).

1 Lorenzo and the Problem of Identity

In the opening scene of the play Lorenzo is shown aiding his cousin the Duke in the midnight abduction of a young Florentine girl. He appears to take delight in acting as Alexandre's procurer, deriving a particular pleasure from witnessing the triumph of vice and corruption. 'Quoi de plus curieux pour le connaisseur', he remarks to the Duke, 'que la débauche à la mamelle?' (I, 1, 11-12). To his mind principles, purity and virtue resemble a thin layer of varnish which disguises the inevitable propensity for vice which lies beneath. Lorenzo possesses a reflective turn of mind and a wounding tongue. His sophisticated cynicism is far removed from the crude sensuality of the Duke. For the latter the satisfaction of physical desire is an end in itself. For Lorenzo this is far from being the case.

In the course of Act One Lorenzo's behaviour is reported and commented on by other characters and in this manner a picture of his complex nature gradually forms in the spectator's mind. We learn that he indulges in riotous behaviour and is no respecter of persons. In his opinion nothing is sacred. He certainly has no qualms about attending a ball dressed as a nun. According to Sire Maurice he is an atheist. News of his previous exploits has spread far beyond the walls of Florence. His conduct has angered the Pope: by bringing the Duke's regime into disrepute he poses a threat to the political strategy of the Vatican. But this is not all. Lorenzo is also suspected of being an informer, of betraying to the Duke the names of his political opponents. He it is who is responsible for the sufferings of the many honest Florentines condemned to exile and banishment. He appears utterly repellent, quite lacking in any moral sense. Significantly, his physical appearance would seem to confirm this. Here is how he is described by the Duke: 'Regardez-moi ce petit corps maigre, ce lendemain d'orgie ambulant. Regardez-moi ces yeux plombés, ces mains fluettes et maladives, à peine assez fermes pour soutenir un éventail, ce visage morne, qui sourit quelquefois, mais qui n'a pas la force de rire' (I, 4, 461-65). As far as the Duke is concerned Lorenzo's weak and sickly appearance is an outward expression of his true being. Such a man is not to be feared for the simple reason that honour and valour form no part of his make-up. The Duke remains blind to the Cardinal's prophetic warning; in Lorenzo he sees only his trusted friend, his companion in debauchery. When, after an exchange of insults, Sire Maurice draws his sword, Lorenzo's reaction is to faint and fall to the ground. But is he really an abject coward? The Cardinal has his doubts and the spectator responds in like manner, wondering whether Lorenzo is feigning and if so, why?

In the course of the play the answer is revealed. Lorenzo is indeed playing a role. He has chosen to assume the character of a debauchee for political reasons. His aim is to serve Florence by ridding the world of the tyrant Alexandre. Only by adopting the mask of the corrupt and dissolute courtier could he gain the Duke's confidence and thus be in a position to assassinate him. But if Lorenzo's motives had originally been pure and idealistic, his course of action has had consequences which he never suspected. The full significance of his role-playing is explained in Act Three. Prior to this, however, Musset emphasises the distance separating the young, idealistic Lorenzo from the cynical, depraved creature he has become. In Act One (I, 6) we witness a conversation between his mother, Marie Soderini, and his aunt, Catherine Ginori. Marie laments the degradation of her son's being. In her dismay we glimpse a mother's inward desolation. She regrets that Lorenzo has abandoned ambition, study and the love of truth. He who could have legitimately aspired to become the ruler of Florence cares nothing for family tradition and civic responsibility. Marie feels betrayed; her son has failed her. Most of all she regrets the passing of Lorenzo's idealism. What has happened to the reader of Plutarch, to the young man who wanted to come to the aid of his fellow men? Even the beauty which Lorenzo once possessed has now vanished from his features. For Marie only disappointment, shame and suffering remain. Yet she does not spurn her son despite his failings, and in a later scene (II, 4) Lorenzo joins his mother and aunt at the Soderini palace. This is the moment when Marie recounts the waking dream in which she pictured the ghost of the young, studious Lorenzo returning home with a book under his arm. There can be no doubt that the dream vividly represents the split, the inward division between present and past, between debauchee and idealist. The spectre disappeared, explains Marie, only when the real Lorenzo returned the following morning. The dream, with its image of the double, forces Lorenzo to confront the problems of selfhood and the unity of the personality. His reaction betrays the power of the dream to body forth the disturbing truths of human existence. 'Qu'avez-vous?', asks Catherine, 'vous tremblez de la tête aux pieds' (II, 4, 1229).

The full nature of Lorenzo's existential predicament is revealed in his long dialogue (III, 3) with Philippe Strozzi, the idealistic and reflective leader of the republicans. Musset's masterstroke lies in showing us a character who, having undergone a life of vice in order to accomplish an act intended to liberate and regenerate society, discovers to his cost that the mask of corruption he had assumed has become a part of his very being. As Lorenzo says to Philippe: 'je me suis fait à mon métier. Le vice a été pour moi un vêtement, maintenant il est collé à ma peau. Je suis vraiment un ruffian, ... Brutus a fait le fou pour tuer Tarquin, et ce qui m'étonne en lui, c'est qu'il n'y ait pas laissé sa raison' (III, 3, 2174-79). The mask of appearance has taken on the substance of reality. But not totally. The presence of the past cannot be erased. Memory cannot be suppressed. Lorenzo remains painfully aware of the person he no longer is: 'Tel que tu me vois, Philippe, j'ai été honnête. J'ai cru à la vertu, à la grandeur humaine, comme un martyr croit à son Dieu' (III, 3, 1987-89). Of the hope and idealism of youth nothing is left except perhaps the remembrance of that which has been lost. The consciousness of the discrepancy between present and past haunts and torments Lorenzo. Had he been able to renounce absolutely his virtuous youth, then some unity, 'albeit a demonic one', might have been vouchsafed him (*25*, p.17). As things are, self-knowledge serves only to shatter his earlier sense of values while increasing the feeling of inner division. Lorenzo has lost his beliefs together with his innocence. Both have withered and died in contact with human reality. Unlike Philippe Strozzi who inhabits a world of pure thought Lorenzo has been sullied by a direct experience of evil:

> Ah! vous avez vécu tout seul, Philippe. Pareil à un fanal éclatant, vous êtes resté immobile au bord de l'océan des hommes et vous avez regardé dans les eaux la réflexion de votre propre lumière. Du fond de votre solitude, vous trouviez l'océan magnifique sous le dais splendide des cieux. Vous ne comptiez pas chaque flot, vous ne jetiez pas la sonde; vous étiez plein de confiance dans l'ouvrage de Dieu. Mais moi, pendant ce temps-là, j'ai plongé — je me suis enfoncé dans cette mer houleuse de la vie — j'en ai parcouru toutes les profondeurs, couvert de ma cloche de verre — tandis que vous admiriez la surface, j'ai vu les débris des naufrages, les ossements et les Léviathans. (III, 3, 2067-77)

Lorenzo's disenchantment with the cause of mankind is complete. He no longer experiences patriotic emotion, no longer feels compassion for suffering humanity. He has donned the mask of vice and now knows men as they really are. Acutely aware of his own degradation he feels distaste, disdain, even revulsion for mankind in general.

The long discussion with Philippe is valuable from another point of view in that it provides detailed information regarding the reasons which originally persuaded Lorenzo to undertake his plan. Here once again the main protagonist's lucidity is worthy of note. Far from explaining his choice of action in terms of a decision arrived at by a process of rational deliberation he underscores the confused, the irrational nature of that irresistible initial impulse:

> Ma jeunesse a été pure comme l'or. Pendant vingt ans de silence, la foudre s'est amoncelée dans ma poitrine; et il

faut que je sois réellement une étincelle du tonnerre, car tout à coup, une certaine nuit que j'étais assis dans les ruines du Colisée antique, je ne sais pourquoi je me levai; je tendis vers le ciel mes bras trempés de rosée, et je jurai qu'un des tyrans de ma patrie mourrait de ma main. J'étais un étudiant paisible, et je ne m'occupais alors que des arts et des sciences, et il m'est impossible de dire comment cet étrange serment s'est fait en moi. (III, 3, 1992-2000)

Lorenzo clearly became obsessed with the image of himself as a new Brutus. He felt sure in his conviction that he had a mission to fulfil. And yet his project lacked focus and direction. Pride, he admits retrospectively, was an important moving force. He did not pursue a definable, attainable goal. Instead he was driven by an overriding desire to play the role of assassin and liberator:

J'ai voulu d'abord tuer Clément VII. Je n'ai pu le faire parce qu'on m'a banni de Rome avant le temps. J'ai recommencé mon ouvrage avec Alexandre. Je voulais agir seul, sans le secours d'aucun homme. Je travaillais pour l'humanité; mais mon orgueil restait solitaire au milieu de tous mes rêves philanthropiques. Il fallait donc entamer par la ruse un combat singulier avec mon ennemi. Je ne voulais pas soulever les masses, ni conquérir la gloire bavarde d'un paralytique comme Cicéron. Je voulais arriver à l'homme, me prendre corps à corps avec la tyrannie vivante, la tuer, porter mon épée sanglante sur la tribune, et laisser la fumée du sang d'Alexandre monter au nez des harangueurs, pour réchauffer leur cervelle ampoulée. (III, 3, 2024-35)

In this speech Musset captures brilliantly Lorenzo's excitable nature, his thirst for violence and his desire to act alone. But Lorenzo is no longer the man he was: self-knowledge has been bought at the cost of the unity of the personality. Looking backward he perceives the confusion which lay at the heart of his own motives. Why then persist with the plan to murder the

Duke? Lorenzo harbours no illusion that the death of Alexandre will bring a new, just society into being. The truth is that Lorenzo now acts for personal, not political, reasons. He explains to Philippe Strozzi that the murder is his only real link with his past: 'veux-tu donc que je rompe le seul fil qui rattache aujourd'hui mon cœur à quelques fibres de mon cœur d'autrefois? ... veux-tu que je laisse mourir en silence l'énigme de ma vie?' (III, 3, 2223-30). Lorenzo's purpose has therefore to be accomplished even though he no longer feels solidarity with any group in society. He cannot define his purpose beyond the brute fact of murder except in personal terms. Yet at the same time he is also conscious that this act, by which he will justify himself in his own eyes, will also serve as his revenge upon a depraved world. Marked indelibly by his life of vice he seeks in turn to leave his mark on mankind, on the body of history. The murder which validates his own existence will simultaneously assert Lorenzo's superiority over his fellow men:

> J'en ai assez de me voir conspué par des lâches sans nom, qui m'accablent d'injures pour se dispenser de m'assommer, comme ils le devraient. J'en ai assez d'entendre brailler en plein vent le bavardage humain; il faut que le monde sache un peu qui je suis, et qui il est. ... Qu'ils m'appellent comme ils voudront, Brutus ou Erostrate, il ne me plaît pas qu'ils m'oublient. Ma vie entière est au bout de ma dague, et que la Providence retourne ou non la tête en m'entendant frapper, je jette la nature humaine à pile ou face sur la tombe d'Alexandre — dans deux jours, les hommes comparaîtront devant le tribunal de ma volonté. (III, 3, 2239-57)

Here we see displayed the contradictory impulses within Lorenzo's character. On the one hand he needs the attention of others who confer upon him a sense of being. On the other he resents strongly standing as an object of contemplation for other consciousnesses. The difficulty resides in the fact that the self is not sufficient unto itself and requires endorsement from without. We catch glimpses of Lorenzo at different stages in his life — as a child, as a bookish schoolboy, as an excitable adolescent, as a debauchee playing the role of Brutus — but what strikes the reader is the discontinuous nature of these states which are perceived as isolated moments. Therein lies the power, the originality and the modernity of *Lorenzaccio*. Past selves are not absorbed within the living continuity of a growing personality. Hence the significance attributed to the idea of the double which becomes an index of self-alienation. We can now grasp the meaning which the Duke's murder holds for Lorenzo. The action, it is hoped, will endorse retrospectively the unity of the personality and invest temporal existence with meaning and direction. The murder will in one sense represent a victory over time, a revelation of the continuity which lies beneath the different masks.

We may now usefully turn to the assassination scene itself (IV, 11). The setting is Lorenzo's bedchamber. The Duke is lying in bed awaiting the arrival of Catherine Ginori with whom he believes he has an assignation. After some brief exchanges Lorenzo strikes the Duke dead with his sword. His immediate reaction is fulfilment and elation: 'Que la nuit est belle! Que l'air du ciel est pur! Respire, respire, cœur navré de joie!' Peace and tranquillity descend on Lorenzo's soul: 'Comme les fleurs des prairies s'entr'ouvrent! O nature magnifique, ô éternel repos!' (IV, 11, 3202-08). Lorenzo seems here to be aware of something akin to the consubstantiality of the self and the world. He experiences a sense of plenitude which dissipates all inward divisions and tensions. This moment is however short-lived. Lorenzo has not been made whole and he does not embark upon a new life. This is clear from the discussion between Lorenzo and Philippe Strozzi when the two men meet in exile in Venice (V, 2). Philippe is filled with joy at the news that the tyrant Alexandre is no more. He still believes that the murder may herald the rebirth of freedom. Lorenzo, however, knows better. Florence will not be regenerated. But the difficulty lies in the fact that with the death of the Duke all meaning and purpose have vanished from Lorenzo's own existence: 'J'étais une machine à meurtre, mais à un meurtre seulement' (V, 6, 3634-35). The sense of fulfilment which followed the murder lasted only a brief moment. It has given way to an agonising awareness of the void within. Henceforth Lorenzo is condemned to experience a desolate inner emptiness: 'je suis plus creux et plus vide qu'une statue de fer-blanc' (V, 6, 3617-18). Having at last accomplished his act he is overcome with a profound sense of *ennui*. Despite his youth he feels old. He knows better than to deceive himself into thinking that the future holds any promise: 'J'aime encore le vin et les femmes; c'est assez, il est vrai, pour faire de moi un débauché, mais ce n'est pas assez pour me donner envie de l'être' (V, 6, 3641-44). Weary with life, Lorenzo knows that only death awaits him. He wanders the streets of Venice paying scant heed to the assassins who dog his steps. A price has been placed on his head but he does not look to his personal safety. Consequently, when he is stabbed from behind and his body dropped ignominiously into the lagoon it is as if Lorenzo has silently acquiesced in the inevitability of his own death, viewing it almost as a form of suicide. Indifferent to life, Lorenzo has become strangely indifferent to his own death.

Lorenzo therefore dies in full knowledge of the ultimate futility, one might say the absurdity, of his own life. He never succeeds in breaking out of his isolation, partly self-imposed, partly enforced from without. Politically he acts alone out of deliberate choice. On a personal level he is not completely isolated: he sustains his friendship with Philippe and experiences love and affection for his mother and aunt. But these relationships do not form a basis for genuine self-fulfilment, for spiritual and emotional growth. In Lorenzo's case there can be no permanent release from self-alienation through contact and emotional exchange with others. Instead he remains entrapped within his own instability, within his difference. His actions serve only to increase his solitude, to sever what links are left between himself and the world of human relations. By his conduct he precipitates his mother's death, thus destroying the only presence which might have consoled him.

The preceding analysis does not, however, exhaust the problems posed by this most enigmatic character. A close reading of the play indicates that the decision to murder the Duke springs from motivations deeper than those examined up to now, hidden motivations which remain largely concealed from Lorenzo himself. In his study *Lorenzaccio ou la difficulté d'être* Bernard Masson contends that the key to the character of the main protagonist is to be found in his acute sense of inferiority. Lorenzo's behaviour is 'tout entière guidée par un *sentiment fondamental d'infériorité*, qu'il s'efforce...de compenser par une surestimation de soi multiforme et irrépressible' (*30*, p.5). Masson, who draws on the theories of Adler, argues his case in some detail. He lays stress on Catherine's remark on seeing her son return from school: 'Ce ne sera jamais un guerrier que mon Renzo' (I, 6, 704-5). Masson concludes that we would be ill-advised to attribute Lorenzo's frail physical appearance solely to the excesses of a life of debauchery. Physical inferiority is rather an intrinsic part of his make-up. To this are added other elements. There is the fact that his rightful position as heir to the Dukedom of Florence has been usurped by Alexandre. There is the added point that Lorenzo, the philosopher, the intellectual, finds himself subservient to a man devoid of culture, taste and finer feelings. Lorenzo is left with a sense of humilition and he compensates for his awareness of his own inferiority by exaggerating his will to power and domination. On one level we note his verbal aggression, the delight he takes in wounding, shocking and scandalising those about him. On a deeper level this psychological mechanism explains his choice of Brutus as a model with whom to identify and informs his vision of himself as a godlike figure passing judgment on all mankind.

Lorenzo is searching for lost innocence in a world from which love is largely absent. His mother represents goodness but an unbridgeable gulf separates maternal love from sexual love. In Lorenzo's eyes most women deserve scorn. They are tainted with evil and corruption. But Lorenzo's attitude towards women cannot simply be subsumed into his general misanthropy. To do so would be to ignore two essential elements. The first refers to a traumatic experience of personal humiliation: 'j'aurais pleuré avec la première fille que j'ai séduite, si elle ne s'était mise à rire' (III, 3, 2121-22). Second, there is what Masson terms Lorenzo's 'fragilité efféminée' (*30*, p.6). In a society which has a clear notion of what constitutes masculinity it is quite apparent that both by his appearance and his behaviour Lorenzo connotes femininity. He is presented as a coward who does not even carry a sword — a traditional symbol of virility. That he should act thus is of course explainable in terms of his plan to gain the Duke's confidence. Yet this is not of itself an adequate explanation. The play points to the reality of Lorenzo's ambivalent sexuality: heterosexual and homosexual elements are simultaneously present in his character. The latter side of his nature is revealed through his relationship with Alexandre. The degree of intimacy shared by the two men is suggested when Lorenzo remarks that in order to win the Duke's trust 'il fallait baiser sur ses lèvres épaisses tous les restes de ses orgies' (III, 3, 2042). He is Alexandre's 'mignon', his Lorenzetta. The Duke refers to him as 'une femmelette' (I, 4, 443). It is also worth recalling that Musset originally intended including a scene portraying Lorenzo and Alexandre asleep together. Lorenzo, however, is not content to play the submissive, female role, and when seen in this light the murder takes on a new dimension of meaning. The killing of the Duke may be understood as an attempt by the masculine side of Lorenzo's nature to assert itself over his feminine side.

Lorenzo's lack of identity of essence, his shifting unstable personae produce in him a psychic dissonance which seeks a discharge of energy, violent in nature. *Lorenzaccio* explores the bond between violence and sexuality. The plan to kill the Duke cannot be satisfactorily explained in terms of revenge, personal or political. The murder answers deeper, more fundamental needs. It is presented in sexual terms as a consummation, a ritual defloration, an unholy marriage. Sexuality and violent death are closely linked in Lorenzo's mind: when he spontaneously compares his sudden desire to kill a tyrant with the experience of falling in love he is in fact isolating a point of fundamental convergence. Unable to coincide with himself, he becomes obsessed with the image of violent, bloody death. This is well illustrated by the scene which depicts Lorenzo and Scoronconcolo rehearsing the murder. The acting has a gruesome reality to it although the loyal servant is at first unaware of the true role he has to play. In this scene the aggressive side of

Lorenzo's character takes over completely. He is swept along by inner forces which he makes no effort to control. It is plainly the experience of killing that Lorenzo desires — rather than the mere fact of the Duke's death. Alexandre has become a beast fit for bloody slaughter, an animal to be disembowelled, cut to pieces, consumed in an almost cannibalistic manner. In his violent anticipatory ecstasy, Lorenzo is carried away to the point of hysteria:

Meurs, infâme! Je te saignerai, pourceau, je te saignerai! Au cœur! au cœur! il est éventré. — Crie donc, frappe donc, tue donc! Ouvre-lui les entrailles! Coupons-le par morceaux, et mangeons, mangeons! J'en ai jusqu'au coude. Fouille dans la gorge, roule-le, roule! Mordons, mordons, et mangeons! *(Il tombe épuisé.)* (III, 1, 1620-25)

The actual murder does not take this form. It is over in a moment. There is just sufficient time for Alexandre to utter the words 'C'est toi, Renzo?' (IV, 11, 3195). Whilst rehearsing the murder with Scoronconcolo, Lorenzo does however speak words which body forth his essential motivations. In a crucial section he directly associates the idea of death with that of marriage: 'O jour de sang, jour de mes noces! O soleil! soleil! il y a assez longtemps que tu es sec comme le plomb; tu te meurs de soif, soleil! son sang t'enivrera' (III, 1, 1629-31). These words suggest that the act is somehow intended to perform a magical, regenerative function. The sun, moreover, is traditionally a masculine symbol and it is quite legitimate to interpret Lorenzo's words as an assertion of virility. As Marie Maclean appositely remarks, we have here the murder-wedding presented as 'a ritual in which blood will both quench the thirst for vengeance and revitalise the masculine principle' (*29*, p.175). By drawing his sword Lorenzo has become an aggressive force. He is transformed into the embodiment of crude animal strength and energy: Scoronconcolo compares his master to a tiger and likens his cry to the sound of lions and panthers roaring in a cave. Once again Lorenzo loses control of his emotions, falls faint and Scoronconcolo has to throw water over his face in order to revive him. Further illustration of Lorenzo's disturbed state of mind is provided in a subsequent scene (IV, 3) where he imagines himself to be the product of some mysterious, monstrous union: 'De quelles entrailles fauves, de quels velus embrassements suis-je donc sorti?' (IV, 3, 2694-95). Lorenzo knows that he can offer no political justification for continuing with his scheme; he makes no attempt to disguise the fact that the Duke has behaved towards him as a friend. Instead, and in order to escape the weight of personal responsibility, he transposes his action onto a mythical plane, investing it with a transcendent meaning. Lorenzo goes so far as to imagine himself as an avenging angel, the instrument of destiny, the tool of divine Providence: 'Suis-je le bras de Dieu? Y a-t-il une nuée au-dessus de ma tête?' (IV, 3, 2712-13).

The pressing need to save Catherine's virtue and protect her from the Duke's advances forces Lorenzo to begin final preparations for the murder. By coming to his aunt's aid he feels he can at least partially redeem himself. But this is not all. By shedding the Duke's blood Lorenzo is seeking something more: he hopes simultaneously to assert his virility and recapture something of his lost innocence. Musset leaves us in no doubt that the act of murder here presented may be perceived as a ritualised seduction or perhaps more accurately as a demonic parody of a wedding night. Lorenzo intends preparing the setting with care, with appropriate attention to detail: 'Je ferai mettre des rideaux blancs à mon lit et un pot de réséda sur ma table' (IV, 1, 2626-27). There is, moreover, a clear parallel between the murder and the play's opening scene. In both cases — at least as far as the Duke is concerned — Lorenzo has been busy at his customary work catering for his master's sensual appetite and desire for nocturnal adventure. On this occasion, however, instead of a compliant mistress the Duke will encounter the sharp edge of Lorenzo's avenging blade. *penis*

The approach of the murder does nothing to incline Lorenzo to view his chosen course of action with more serenity. On the contrary he remains excitable, susceptible to sudden changes of mood. His powerful soliloquy (IV, 9) shows him once again projecting himself into the future, imagining a conversation with

Alexandre. He wonders whether a torch should be left burning in the bedchamber. At first he hesitates, but then, impatient for violence, he decides that the light should not be removed:

> Je lui dirai que c'est un motif de pudeur, et j'emporterai la lumière — cela se fait tous les jours — une nouvelle mariée, par exemple, exige cela de son mari pour entrer dans la chambre nuptiale, et Catherine passe pour très vertueuse. ... Non! non! je n'emporterai pas la lumière. — J'irai droit au cœur; il se verra tuer... Sang du Christ! on se mettra demain aux fenêtres. (IV, 9, 3052-75)

After expressing anger at the weakness of the republicans, Lorenzo thinks of death. He is temporarily overcome with lassitude, with a sense of *taedium vitae*. But the sound of the clock striking interrupts this mood and reminds him of his purpose. Once again his instability is manifest: Lorenzo is seized by an irresistible desire to dance. In the final lines of the soliloquy the theme of sexuality returns with force: 'Eh, mignon, eh, mignon! mettez vos gants neufs, un plus bel habit que cela, tra la la! faites-vous beau, la mariée est belle. Mais, je vous le dis à l'oreille, prenez garde à son petit couteau' (IV, 9, 3121-24). Here Lorenzo is casting himself in the role of the bride but in the event the bride will become the bridegroom. There is already a suggestion that roles are to be reversed. The Duke will wear his new gloves and fine clothes; Lorenzo will be armed with a weapon. Marie Maclean observes that at this point Lorenzo 'has succeeded in temporarily reintegrating his divided self ... he is both male and female, both the sacrifice and the sacrificer' (*29*, p.179). When he kills the Duke Lorenzo overcomes his sense of inner humiliation and asserts his masculinity more fully. By a subtle use of spatial relationships, Musset signals that Alexandre is no longer the dominant partner. When Lorenzo enters the Duke is lying on the bed impatiently awaiting the arrival of Catherine. He no longer has his chain-mail to protect him and Lorenzo has ensured that he is unable to draw his sword. Lorenzo is in command and when he strikes — using an untarnished blade appropriate for a ritual — the Duke is

powerless to resist, 'symbolically castrated' in the terminology
of Marie Maclean (*29*, p.179). The Duke is now at one and the
same time bride and sacrificial victim. The union between the
two men is sealed in blood. As Lorenzo says to Scoronconcolo:
'Regarde, il m'a mordu au doigt. Je garderai jusqu'à la mort
cette bague sanglante, inestimable diamant' (IV, 11, 3199-200).

But the mood of elation which follows the doing of the deed is
short-lived. The assassination is a failure in political terms: the
shedding of the blood of Alexandre does not mark the
purification of Florence. No new order is established. On a
personal level Lorenzo discovers that by committing himself to
action he achieves no real delivrance, attains no revelation of
value or meaning. Neither for that matter does the murder
integrate successfully and durably the masculine and feminine
aspects of his nature. What is more, he knows that the murder
cannot be repeated. Loreanzo's story is a tale of failure. For him
there remains only the release of death.

2 The Social World

Musset depicts a world where vice and corruption rule supreme, where justice is denied and where traditional values are spurned. Florence has become Alexandre's plaything. The Duke exercises power in a quite arbitrary fashion and those who dare oppose him can expect banishment if not death. The people groan under the yoke of oppression. They suffer at the hands of the German soldiery whose function it is to assure the maintenance of the Duke's misrule. The opening scenes swiftly and persuasively convey the impression of a city in moral decline, a city without beliefs and values, far removed from the noble, freedom-loving Florence of the past. In Maffio's words the city has become 'une forêt pleine de bandits, pleine d'empoisonneurs et de filles déshonorées' (I, 1, 72-73). On the evidence provided by the play this seems an accurate description. Florence in 1536 is a city without an ordering principle or ideal. Money is all-powerful. In this society a mother will sell her daughter's virtue for a thousand ducats. The sorry state of the city is further underlined by the Goldsmith and the Silk Merchant. It is morning and these two members of the mercantile middle classes have been kept awake by the music issuing forth from the ball held to celebrate the coming marriage of Nasi's daughter. The Silk Merchant has had his sleep disturbed but is not too displeased. He finds solace in the fact that the nobles do, after all, purchase their fine cloth at his establishment. The Goldsmith, on the other hand, is quite acerbic in his criticisms. He reminds his friend that many of his aristocratic customers leave their bills unpaid. His attitude, however, is not one of personal recrimination. As a man of principle he speaks out against the dissipation and licence of the court. Without hesitation he castigates the conduct of the Duke. For the Goldsmith does not delude himself. He knows only too well that it is the exploitation of the people which guarantees the life of the court. His is the voice of moral censure joined with popular resentment: the Medici are a cancer slowly devouring the body of Florence. But what is to be done? How can the process of decline be halted and reversed? The failure of Lorenzo's plan to regenerate Florence has been charted in the preceding chapter. The play, however, describes two other attempts at transforming the present order of things. These are the sub-plots which involve, respectively, Ricciarda Cibo and Philippe Strozzi. These strategies parallel and illuminate the course of action taken by the main protagonist.

When we first meet Ricciarda Cibo she is saying goodbye to her husband, the Marquis, who is about to spend a week away from his family on his estates. The leavetaking is tearful and tender. Ricciarda appears to be without question an affectionate and devoted wife. She is also no friend of the Duke. Her political sympathies lie with the opposition. This emerges from the exchanges between Ricciarda and her brother-in-law, the scheming Cardinal Cibo. She is forthright in her condemnation of the order which the Cardinal supports. In Florence, she declares, 'la débauche [sert] d'entremetteuse à l'esclavage, et secoue ses grelots sur les sanglots du peuple' (I, 3, 354-55). But having established that Ricciarda is a loving spouse whose heart is in the right place, Musset immediately shatters our illusions by having the Cardinal intercept a secret missive in which the Duke declares his amorous intentions towards the Marquise. Our surprise at this revelation is not shared by the Cardinal who has long been aware of Alexandre's attempts to seduce Ricciarda. The spectator, on the other hand, is left wondering whether Ricciarda is a paragon of republican virtue or a deceitful adultress. In fact, like Lorenzo, the Marquise has decided to assume a mask for political reasons. She is willing to sacrifice her virtue and her reputation since she believes that as the Duke's mistress she will be able to influence the course of events of state. The first part of her plan succeeds admirably: in her husband's absence she yields to the Duke's advances. Beyond that, however, her venture is an abject failure. She has no success whatsoever in communicating her passionate political idealism to a lover who is only interested in her as a sexual conquest. She urges the Duke to emulate '[le] Père de la Patrie', to declare Florence independent, to redeem himself in the eyes of posterity (III, 6, 2364). But the Duke is indifferent both to her patriotism and to her attempts to transform him into an heroic ruler. The Marquise's wordy speeches bore him. He is left unaltered by the experience of her love. But did her plan ever really stand a chance of succeeding? Surely it was built upon erroneous assumptions, upon a complete misunderstanding of the man it was designed to influence. Alexandre could never have fulfilled the role of leader as imagined by the Marquise. What is more, Ricciarda's motives are themselves not without ambiguity:

> Est-ce que j'aime Alexandre? Non, je ne l'aime pas, non, assurément; j'ai dit que non dans ma confession, et je n'ai pas menti. Pourquoi Laurent est-il à Massa? Pourquoi le duc me presse-t-il? Pourquoi ai-je répondu que je ne voulais plus le voir? pourquoi? — Ah! pourquoi y a-t-il dans tout cela un aimant, un charme inexplicable qui m'attire? *(Elle ouvre sa fenêtre.)* Que tu es belle, Florence, mais que tu es triste! Il y a là plus d'une maison où Alexandre est entré la nuit, couvert de son manteau; c'est un libertin, je le sais. — Et pourquoi est-ce que tu te mêles à tout cela, toi, Florence? Qui est-ce donc que j'aime? Est-ce toi? Est-ce lui? (II, 3, 1169-79)

Far from signalling certainty of purpose Ricciarda's words betoken a disturbing confusion of motives. She is at heart a naïve woman, unable fully to understand, control and direct her own impulses. She is plainly physically attracted to the Duke. She is thus no more successful than Lorenzo in preserving the purity of her original intention. Unlike Lorenzo, however, she survives the failure of her dangerous attempt at role-playing. Preferring frank disclosure to becoming the instrument of the Cardinal she openly confesses her adultery to the husband she has wronged. The latter would appear to view his wife's infidelity with remarkable equanimity since near the end of the play (V, 3) the couple walk across the stage, arm in arm. Is this an example of the healing power of loving forgiveness? The scene could be viewed in quite a different light. An alternative interpretation is perhaps indicated by the fact that the characters do not speak. Ricciarda has not merely failed; she is now silently acquiescing in the reimposition of the old order in Florence. If private happiness has been achieved it has been bought at the cost of abandoning the hope of contributing to the public good.

Philippe Strozzi is a much rounder character than Ricciarda Cibo. He possesses a potentially tragic dimension. As leader of the republicans he is the focus of opposition to the Duke's rule. He embodies the aristocratic resistance to Alexandre, he exemplifies that idea of Florence which animates the other characters. He is, in the words of the Goldsmith, 'le plus brave homme de Florence' (I, 2, 152). Philippe is an idealist, a man who believes profoundly in mankind and in the ultimate triumph of good over evil. But his idealism does not spring from a direct contact with human reality in its many forms. Humanitarian platitudes flow freely from Philippe's lips since he has not had to compromise with the ways of the world. His conception of what society should be like is grounded in a particular image of the heroic past: 'Je me suis courbé sur des livres, et j'ai rêvé pour ma patrie ce que j'admirais dans l'antiquité' (II, 5, 1462-63). He possesses a reflective, philosophical turn of mind. But whilst his idealistic faith in man has been nurtured in studious isolation he is not immune to doubt and despair as his soliloquy at the opening of Act II indicates:

Quand l'éducation des basses classes sera-t-elle assez forte pour empêcher les petites filles de rire lorsque leurs parents pleurent! La corruption est-elle donc une loi de nature? Ce qu'on appelle la vertu, est-ce donc l'habit du dimanche qu'on met pour aller à la messe? ... Pauvre humanité! quel nom portes-tu donc? celui de ta race, ou celui de ton baptême? Et nous autres, vieux rêveurs, quelle tache originelle avons-nous lavée sur la face humaine depuis quatre ou cinq mille ans que nous jaunissons avec nos livres? ... Que le bonheur des hommes ne soit qu'un rêve, cela est pourtant dur; que le mal soit irrévocable, éternel, impossible à changer... non! (II, 1, 797-816)

In these lines we see how, when tested, Philippe's optimistic world view fails to carry conviction. His confidence momentarily evaporates as he is overcome by an awareness of the all-pervasiveness of evil which appears destined to thwart all man's pitiful attempts to improve his lot.

The underlying inadequacies of Philippe's idealism are exposed during his long conversation with Lorenzo. The relationship between the two men recalls that of a father and son. There is, moreover, a deeper bond. Had not Lorenzo once espoused the very aspirations which still form the creed of the older man? There is here a bizarre reversal of roles since it is Lorenzo, and not Philippe, who speaks with the voice of age and experience: 'C'est parce que je vous vois tel que j'ai été, et sur le point de faire ce que j'ai fait, que je vous parle ainsi' (III, 3, 2079-80). Despite his passing doubts Philippe remains an idealist at heart. He refuses to accept as definitive the pessimism of the younger man: 'Je crois à tout ce que tu appelles des rêves; je crois à la vertu, à la pudeur et à la liberté' (III, 3, 2100-01). Philippe's view of man is drawn from books, not life. Lorenzo endeavours to explain to Philippe that historians and history books should not be relied upon: 'le tort des livres et des historiens est de nous montrer [les hommes] différents de ce qu'ils sont' (III, 3, 2081-82). In his youth Lorenzo had been a fervent reader of Plutarch but since then he has plumbed the murky depths of existence. Most importantly, he has learnt that to try to make one's ideals a reality leads to disastrous consequences. He urges Philippe not to act, not to seek to bring about the happiness of mankind, but rather to allow him, Lorenzo, to rid Florence of the Duke. His efforts are, however, in vain.

Philippe is the acknowledged leader of the republican faction. He is a respected man and the impression is given that without his support no attempt to oust the Duke is likely to succeed. As the exiles leave Florence for Rome, Pisa or Venice their thoughts turn to the man who remains their last hope: 'Que Philippe vive longtemps! tant qu'il y aura un cheveu sur sa tête, la liberté de l'Italie n'est pas morte' (I, 6, 781-82). Yet Philippe does not organise opposition in a purposeful manner. Even after his daughter's murder he refuses to contemplate insurrection and has no truck with the idea of relying upon the intervention of a foreign power. When he does counsel direct action it is not because he judges the moment opportune but because he is stirred by strong feelings of a more personal nature. One noteworthy instance occurs when Philippe is filled with concern over the fate of his son Pierre who has left to take revenge on Salviati. Paternal emotion awakens in Philippe the realisation that his sense of values ought long since to have commanded him to seek positive remedies for the ills of his compatriots: 'Les murs criaient vengeance autour de moi, et je me bouchais les oreilles pour m'enfoncer dans mes méditations — il a fallu que la tyrannie vînt me frapper au visage pour me faire dire: Agissons!' (II, 5, 1463-67). Philippe requires the stimulus of direct involvement in order to be galvanised into action but once the immediate crisis is resolved his concern for the public good recedes into the background. Moreover, once he does commit himself to action he rapidly loses his composure. The leader of the republicans is transformed into an excitable human being, unable to maintain his grasp of the situation which confronts him. Additional evidence is provided by Act III sc. 2. Philippe is in conversation with Pierre. The latter cannot contain his anger; he has discovered that the detestable Salviati has not got his just deserts after all. We are told that a conspiracy against the Duke is afoot, a rebellion in which Pierre will join forces with the Pazzi. Philippe's initial reaction is predictable: he urges restraint. How can anyone contemplate taking action without having first drawn up a detailed plan of campaign? On this occasion Philippe is offering sound advice since the plan is hopelessly ill-conceived. He cannot, however, control his emotions and his attachment to a sense of family honour prompts him in the end to share Pierre's enthusiasm for action. Yet another example of the abdication of the reasoning faculty before the power of strong personal feeling occurs when Philippe rejects Lorenzo's plea not to act. His words are unambiguous: 'Tu peux avoir raison, mais il faut que j'agisse; je vais rassembler mes parents' (III, 3, 2263-64). By calling his clan together Philippe is unwittingly setting the scene for the murder of his beloved daughter. Philippe's reaction to Louise's death is in itself instructive; griefstricken, he immediately abandons all resolve to act. Distressed, distraught, in a state of shock, he is unable to cope with the tragedy which has befallen him: 'J'en ai assez, voyez-vous; j'en ai autant que j'en puis porter' (III, 7, 2565-66). His sole concern is now the burial of his daughter's body. Having finally been moved to take practical steps he finds Louise dead and his two sons in prison. A broken man, he leaves for Venice. But by so doing he leaves the way open for Pierre's rash attempt to overthrow the Duke. Pierre acts but he too fails; only two German soldiers are killed in what Alexandre disparagingly dismisses as the Strozzi's little revolution. And yet, despite everything, Philippe seems to learn little from the experiences he undergoes — on hearing of the Duke's murder he still hails Lorenzo as a new Brutus. The lessons of failure have not been learnt. In the words of Henri Lefebvre Philippe Strozzi represents 'l'échec de l'idéalisme humaniste et libéral devant la brutale violence' (*14*, p.118).

Lorenzo kills the Duke but is left irrevocably tarnished by the life which he has led. As I indicated in the last chapter his death contains no revelation of meaning if not the meaninglessness of existence itself. Ricciarda Cibo embarks upon a politically motivated adultery only to discover the force of her own carnal nature. Pierre, courageous but headstrong, ultimately sells his honour to the king of France in order to further his personal fortunes. Philippe Strozzi, a figure of proven integrity, discovers that action leads to disaster. Demonstrably, devotion to an ideal, however just, is not enough. But to what cause is this failure attributable? to insufficient preparation? to poor execution? The play in fact raises a more disturbing question since it suggests that all ideals are corrupted once they leave the realm of thought and brave the test of concrete realisation. Purity of intention cannot be preserved from the inevitable compromise with reality. The spirit is enslaved by the flesh and all attempts to make ideals a reality appear doomed to failure.

Lorenzaccio portrays not only the power but also the fascination of evil. Mere bystanders fall victim to its charm. The reader recalls the reaction of the students quite overcome by delight at the spectacle of the guests leaving Nasi's ball: 'Rose, vert, bleu, j'en ai plein les yeux; la tête me tourne' (I, 2, 242-43). The nocturnal goings-on draw disapproving comments from a middle-class passer-by but his wife responds in a totally different way. Far from sharing her husband's reproachful attitude she expresses admiration tinged with envy: 'Comme tout est illuminé! danser encore à l'heure qu'il est, c'est là une jolie fête. — On dit que le duc y est. ... Ah! la belle robe! Hélas! tout cela coûte très cher, et nous sommes bien pauvres à la maison' (I, 2, 207-15). In *Lorenzaccio* a mere moment suffices for corruption to seize hold of the soul, for a complete reversal of values to take place. The fate of Maffio's sister, 'corrompue, devenue une fille publique en une nuit', is exemplary (II, 1, 796-97). Social life in general is revealed to be a hypocritical masquerade. Principles, beliefs, ideals, all evaporate when the overriding claims of self-interest make themselves manifest. A fine illustration is the comic scene in which Lorenzo tricks Bindo Altoviti and Venturi into showing us that the real driving force behind their actions is their passion for self-advancement. Musset prepares us by first introducing Bindo as an apparently sincere republican who is fast losing patience with Lorenzo's failure to declare himself openly. At that moment the Duke enters and Lorenzo quite unexpectedly begs Alexandre to grant favours to his loyal and devoted subjects, Bindo and Venturi. Unaware of Lorenzo's heavy irony the Duke swiftly complies with this request. Bindo is appointed ambassador to Rome. Probity vanishes as ambition triumphs. The few words spoken by Bindo to Venturi need no commentary: 'Que diable veux-tu que je fasse? Je suis nommé' (II, 4, 1321).

In Musset's play religious as well as social values are thoroughly debased and perverted. The Catholic Church has ceased to be the concrete embodiment of religious truths. Instead it has become 'un lieu de débauche' (II, 3, 1071). Religion, like all other forms of collective life, has been degraded. In the words of Ricciarda Cibo, 'nous sommes dans un triste temps pour toutes les choses saintes!' (I, 3, 330-31). Religion has become a spectacle, an excuse for financial gain. The Church cares precious little for the Christian message, for

the spiritual dimension of man. Organised religion is an
instrument of the established order. The Pope possesses no
moral authority. What right, asks Alexandre, has a man like the
Pope to complain of Lorenzo's conduct and demand his return
to Rome: 'Alexandre Farnèse est un plaisant garçon! Si la
débauche l'effarouche, que diable fait-il de son bâtard, le cher
Pierre Farnèse, qui traite si joliment l'évêque de Fano?' (I, 4,
421-23). The Pope is in league with Charles V, the Holy Roman
Emperor. Together they hold the real power and oppress the
people. The Duke is their instrument, their puppet. Power in
Florence lies not with Alexandre but with Cardinal Cibo. Whilst
Cardinal Baccio Valori acts openly as papal emissary to the
Florentine court Cibo operates mysteriously, quietly, and is all
the more effective in his master's service precisely because he has
no official role. Cibo is endowed with a Machiavellian turn of
mind and is willing to accept all methods provided that they
bring success: 'Qu'il [le duc] épuise sa force contre des ombres
d'hommes gonflés d'une ombre de puissance, je serai l'anneau
invisible qui l'attachera, pieds et poings liés, à la chaîne de fer
dont Rome et César tiennent les deux bouts' (II, 3, 1039-42).

The Cardinal is a perceptive reader of minds, attentive to the
mood of those around him. He knows from the start that
Lorenzo is a serious threat to the Duke. A subtle user of words
and manipulator of people he exploits his position and the
illusion of sanctity he projects in order to advance his own aims.
He is unscrupulous, hypocritical and power-seeking. The end
always justifies the means. This prelate is perfectly at home in
the depraved world in which he moves. He views with indulgence
the fact that the Duke wore a nun's habit: 'le duc est jeune,
marquise, et gageons que cet habit coquet des nonnes lui allait à
ravir' (I, 3, 342-43). There are moments when he strikes a note
of unctuous hypocrisy worthy of Molière's Tartuffe. Immoral
actions are condoned provided they serve his interests: 'Rien
n'est un péché quand on obéit à un prêtre de l'Eglise romaine' (I,
3, 364-65). The prospect of blackmailing his own sister-in-law in
no way disconcerts the Cardinal. Angry and exasperated,
Ricciarda legitimately wonders whether there are any limits to
the Cardinal's corruption: 'Pour gouverner Florence en

gouvernant le duc, vous vous feriez femme tout à l'heure, si vous pouviez' (IV, 4, 2829-30). The Cardinal — who is likened to a vulture — epitomises that inversion of values which lies at the very heart of *Lorenzaccio*. He it is who triumphs at the close of the play with the election of Côme. Ruled by demonic forces he is a figure devoid of all redeeming features: 'César a vendu son ombre au diable; cette ombre impériale se promène, affublée d'une robe rouge, sous le nom de Cibo' (IV, 4, 2726-28). Even in the depraved world portrayed in the play the Cardinal's malevolent genius commands our attention. To some degree a concession to the Romantic taste for the 'grey eminence', Cibo is nevertheless a dominating figure in his own right, a memorable representation of unprincipled lust for power.

The Florence of the Duke and the Cardinal is therefore a city in full moral decline. Maffio, in his vain attempt to save his sister's honour, swears by 'ce qu'il y a de vrai et de sacré au monde' (I, 1, 65-66). But the true and the holy have been debased and perverted to such an extent that they have all but disappeared from the world portrayed by Musset. The Duke is no more than a common criminal with no respect for human life; the Pope is a debauchee. The regime's survival is ensured by expelling from the collective body those who threaten it and by encouraging those citizens who remain to become willing participants in the general web of corruption. There no longer exists a set of shared values to which the individual can adhere. Faith and justice have become meaningless concepts. Social relations are subordinated to monetary exchange. Money manifestly erodes belief, saps conviction. It is a corrosive force which dissolves traditional moral values. The Duke may purchase everything he desires, from a new horse to a girl's virtue. What could be more appropriate than that Lorenzo should die at the hands of a killer seeking a reward? The ruling order has no need of truth, of honesty — the word 'honnête' often carries an ironic charge in *Lorenzaccio* — for what it really seeks is the perpetuation of its own power. The Goldsmith may well speak of 'l'honnête homme qui travaille pour sa famille' (I, 2, 143-44) but can such a person exist in the world described in the play? Indeed the Goldsmith is himself an interesting case. He resents the Duke's tyranny but his professional existence is enmeshed in a network of social relations which supports the existing power structure. A merchant may give vent to his criticism of the established order but he remains economically dependent upon that self-same order. The merchants exist in a position of dependency with regard to the aristocracy, a social class which simultaneously attracts and repels them.

Florence is a city acquiescing in the destruction of its own soul. But as Lorenzo, in his depraved condition, still remembers his original purity, so the Florentines look back to the time when Florence was a great republic. The characters move through a dangerous, a treacherous urban landscape. But, even so, the memory of the collective past cannot be erased. Names of people and places summon up recollections of a unified, ordered social world. The characters who oppose the Duke all consider that it is their duty to liberate Florence and restore the city to its former glory. Patriotism, however, is no simple emotion and the wish to free Florence from tyranny is not the clear objective it may at first seem to be. We have already seen how the republican idealism of Ricciarda Cibo becomes confused with love of the person of Alexandre. There remains a further point to be noted. For is it not significant that the Marquise shows no sign of calling into question the Duke's right to exercise power over his citizens? This potential heroine of the republican cause is strangely enamoured of the Duke's almost divine ability to make his wishes a reality by imposing his will on 'le pâle troupeau des hommes' (III, 6, 2341).

The republicans share the expectation that the removal of the Duke from power will bring about a return to the glories of the Florentine past. Yet for all their brave talk of freedom and justice they are more concerned with sectional class interest than with the well-being of the people as a whole. Philippe, whose mind naturally looks for analogies in Roman history, conceives of Florence essentially as a political entity whose citizens are to be freed from the tyrant's rule (see 35). The revolution which he hopes for is not a mass uprising or insurrection but rather action taken on their own by the noble families. In Philippe's eyes the Florence of the future, like the Florence of the past, will be an oligarchy. What matters above all else is family pride and reputation: 'Nous sommes tout autant que les Médicis, les Ruccellaï tout autant, les Aldobrandini et vingt autres. ... Il y a à Florence quatre-vingts palais, et de chacun d'eux sortira une troupe pareille à la nôtre, quand la Liberté y frappera' (III, 7, 2483-502). Bindo Altoviti's convictions are not that dissimilar. By espousing republicanism he is endeavouring to recover lost privileges: 'Toutes les grandes familles voient bien que le despotisme des Médicis n'est ni juste ni tolérable. De quel droit laisserions-nous s'élever paisiblement cette maison orgueilleuse sur les ruines de nos privilèges?' (II, 4, 1259-62).

To view Florence simply as a city to be liberated would be an oversimplification. It would be more accurate to say that the city functions as an ideal in people's minds, inspiring their thoughts, guiding their destinies. It is the focus of the characters' desires and aspirations. In *Lorenzaccio* Florence has the status of a mythical figure, a mother figure, loved and revered by her citizens. 'J'aime ma mère Florence' declares Tebaldeo (II, 2, 1009). But for many Florence is no longer a life-giving, life-sustaining force. Instead we are presented with a further illustration of the theme of love corrupted. The city's condition exemplifies a people's collective moral decline. Florence has been violated, defiled by Alexandre's violence and lust; it has become, in Lorenzo's words a 'mauvais lieu' (II, 2, 962). The mother figure has been debased, transformed into a lady of easy virtue. Florence is now a cruel mother, drinking the blood of her children with indifference. Eloquent in their despair the exiles curse the city they leave behind them:

LE PREMIER BANNI. — Adieu, Florence, peste de l'Italie; adieu, mère stérile, qui n'as plus de lait pour tes enfants.
LE SECOND. — Adieu, Florence, la bâtarde, spectre hideux de l'antique Florence; adieu, fange sans nom.
TOUS LES BANNIS. — Adieu, Florence! maudites soient les mamelles de tes femmes! maudits soient tes sanglots! maudites les prières de tes églises, le pain de tes blés, l'air de tes rues! Malédiction sur la dernière goutte de ton sang corrompu! (I, 6, 787-94)

Where then does goodness lie in the sombre moral landscape of *Lorenzaccio*? Three characters instantly come to mind. First there is Lorenzo's mother, Marie Soderini. However, she dies, unable to bear the shame of what her son has become. Second, we have Louise Strozzi. She represents the alliance of youth and beauty, innocence and virtue. But she too meets her death. Finally, there is the figure of Lorenzo's young aunt, Catherine Ginori. She is linked directly to the divine order of nature, to that sustaining force which is excluded from the cruel urban world in which the drama unfolds. Virtuous and proud, she survives the fall of the Duke and will — so Lorenzo hopes — give birth to honest offspring. She remains nevertheless an isolated, fragile element in the general pattern of corruption. For in Musset's world can any woman resist indefinitely the powerful temptation of vice? We would be wise to mark well Lorenzo's words: 'J'allais corrompre Catherine — Je crois que je corromprais ma mère, si mon cerveau le prenait à tâche' (IV, 5, 2887-88). Marie, Catherine and Louise represent a horizon of value, an area of experience which exists on the margin of the play's moral universe, an area which is always under threat. Can paradise lost ever be regained in a world where attempts to make ideals a reality end in compromise and defeat?

But if action fails, if the Duke's blood fails to regenerate Florence, is there not another path to follow? Can artistic creation provide an answer to the moral problems posed by *Lorenzaccio*? In other words, is it possible for man to redeem the fallen world through art, to transcend time by transforming experiential reality into an enduring work of beauty? It is noteworthy that Musset has chosen to include in his cast of characters an artist, Tebaldeo Frescia. The young painter fulfils an obvious dramatic function since Lorenzo is able to steal the Duke's chain-mail shirt while Alexandre is having his portrait painted. Tebaldeo, however, is equally important on account of the ideas which he puts forward. When we first meet him he is in conversation with Lorenzo and Cardinal Valori on the steps of a church. Here is a young man with philosophical and artistic interests but who, unlike Lorenzo, has kept his enthusiasm and idealism intact. A disciple of Raphael, Tebaldeo unhesitatingly associates art with religious experience, describing himself as 'un desservant bien humble de la sainte religion de la peinture' (II, 2, 910-11). He is an obviously sympathetic character, showing sincerity, directness and an independence of spirit. His beliefs are unshaken, his youth unsullied, his values confidently proclaimed. Tebaldeo carries with him a painting of the Campo Santo which he shows to his two interlocutors. Valori, man of the Church, speaks words of encouragement. Lorenzo, provoked by the presence of faith and belief, tricks and traps Tebaldeo, playing verbal games with him, indulging in irony and sarcasm at the painter's expense. He asks Tebaldeo to paint a picture of the courtesan Mazzafirra in all her nakedness. Tebaldeo refuses. He does, however, agree to produce a painting of Florence. Lorenzo has his riposte at the ready: 'Pourquoi donc ne peux-tu peindre une courtisane, si tu peux peindre un mauvais lieu?' (II, 2, 961-62). At this point Tebaldeo expresses his profound conviction that great art is born of suffering:

> Une blessure sanglante peut engendrer la corruption dans le corps le plus sain. Mais des gouttes précieuses du sang de ma mère [Florence] sort une plante odorante qui guérit tous les maux. L'art, cette fleur divine, a quelquefois besoin du fumier pour engraisser le sol et le féconder. ... Les nations paisibles et heureuses ont quelquefois brillé d'une clarté pure, mais faible. ... L'enthousiasme est frère de la souffrance. ... Je plains les peuples malheureux, mais je crois en effet qu'ils font les grands artistes. Les champs de bataille font pousser les moissons, les terres corrompues engendrent le blé céleste. (II, 2, 969-93)

Tebaldeo's argument is rooted in an awareness of solidarity in suffering which permits the artist to forge a work of beauty. He is under no illusions concerning the evils and dangers of Florence: he goes about armed with a dagger and vows that should the Duke attack him he would not hesitate to kill his assailant. But at the same time Tebaldeo also serves to illustrate the artist's independence from political constraints and considerations. When Lorenzo asks bluntly whether he is a republican or a lover of princes his reply indicates his fundamental attachment to the notion of artistic freedom: 'Je suis artiste; j'aime ma mère et ma maîtresse' (II, 2, 1028). Should we conclude that art is the only true sanctuary, the only successful way to embody the ideal in the real? Tebaldeo's words have been understood along these lines but they also admit a rather different interpretation. First, there is the question of the extent to which Tebaldeo's idealism is simply youthful naïvety. How independent can an artist be who accepts commissions from the rich and powerful? By agreeing to paint the Duke Tebaldeo not only aids unwittingly Lorenzo's plans; he also accepts to represent on canvas a reality far more horrendous than a naked courtesan. This point is surely underlined by the sitting itself (II, 6) where the Duke talks casually of violence and murder and produces a feeling of discomfiture in Tebaldeo. The notion that art, born of suffering, can redeem reality certainly appealed to Musset but in *Lorenzaccio* the weight of the evidence comes down against this view. Indeed it would be difficult to disagree with D. Sices' observation that the dream of art vanishes from the play when Tebaldeo makes his last appearance (*17*, p.165). The references to art contained in the remainder of the text do nothing to support Tebaldeo's creed. Is art a satisfactory response to the problem of existence? When Lorenzo notices some men cutting stones beneath the portico of a church he makes a revealing comment: 'Il paraît que ces hommes sont courageux avec les pierres. Comme ils coupent! comme ils enfoncent! Ils font un crucifix; avec quel courage ils le clouent! Je voudrais voir que leur cadavre de marbre les prît tout d'un coup à la gorge' (IV, 9, 3114-16). Might not these remarks be taken to imply that art in general and sacred art in particular is a retreat from reality, an act of weakness, not strength? Neither should we ignore the scene (V, 5) near the close of the play where the two pedants discuss a sonnet whilst their young charges aim kicks at each other. The first tutor — the author of the sonnet in question — has trimmed his sails to the political wind by penning a poem in honour of freedom and the republic: 'Vous serez peut-être étonné que moi, qui ai commencé par chanter la monarchie en quelque sorte, je semble cette fois chanter la république' (V, 5, 3577-79). The irony is of course that by shifting his allegiance the absurd sonneteer has in fact made a serious miscalculation! In this manner the play, in the words of D. Sices, 'closes with a glimpse of the artist's surrender, his voluntary and cowardly adaptation to a world he is powerless either to influence or to comprehend' (*17*, pp.167-68).

The analysis of the social world has revealed the bleakness of Musset's vision. Neither art nor action is capable of redeeming the world of men. Love, which implies the opening up of the possibility of perfection, cannot survive in an environment in which everything conspires so strongly against it. A deep pessimism pervades *Lorenzaccio*. Nowhere is this more apparent than in Musset's vision of history.

3 Politics and History

The action of *Lorenzaccio* has as its setting Renaissance Florence but the play is permeated by the political atmosphere of France, and particularly of Paris, in the early 1830s. An essential part of the play's meaning is lost if, whilst doing justice to the universality of Musset's message, we pay inadequate attention to the circumstances in which the text was produced. When viewed in this light *Lorenzaccio* comes to be seen as a response to recent French history and the revolutionary tradition, the key element being the French Revolution of July 1830. A brief outline of the events of 1830 together with a sketch of their causes and consequences will serve as a reminder of the background.

In July 1830 barricades appeared on the streets of Paris and the government of the day was overthrown by a violent popular uprising. The Restoration, the regime which had held sway since the defeat of Napoleon, passed into history and Charles X, the last Bourbon king of France, was compelled to take flight. The Restoration sought to put the clock back to the world of the Ancien Régime. From the start it was a reactionary administration but its conservative character grew more pronounced when Charles X came to the throne in 1824 after the death of Louis XVIII. Charles was very much a man of the right, a staunch believer in the need for a close alliance of throne and altar. During his reign the influence of the clergy increased considerably. The passing in 1825 of a law making sacrilege a crime punishable by death gives a fair impression of the regime's character. Charles was not, however, an astute politician and his support of the Church produced a revival of anticlericalism. As the years passed the opposition grew in strength. The men of the liberal opposition had their intellectual leaders: the philosopher Cousin and the historian Guizot; and their newspaper, *Le Globe*. They were united in their support of the Greeks in their struggle for national independence against the Turks. Political

agitation increased as the economic situation deteriorated.
Guizot's political society, 'Aide-toi, le ciel t'aidera', spread
liberal propaganda which was favourably received. The
opposition achieved successes in the elections of November
1827. The national mood was clearly changing. Yet Charles still
resisted compromise and was determined to retain full control.
In August 1829 a new ministry was formed under Polignac but
this proved to be singularly ineffectual at a time when the left
was developing a political organisation. Fresh elections took
place in June and July 1830 and on this occasion the opposition
carried the day despite the narrowness of the franchise. Nevertheless Charles found this outcome totally unacceptable and on
26 July 1830 there appeared the Ordinances imposing press
censorship, dissolving parliament and proposing new limitations
to the franchise. In the eyes of many, such authoritarianism was
the last straw. Charles had shown himself to be incapable of
comprehending the nation's legitimate aspirations. Street
disturbances began in Paris on 27 July and these soon grew into
a general insurrection. The three days' fighting which followed
entered the mythology of revolutionary France as 'Les Trois
Glorieuses'. The success of the popular movement could not be
doubted. The Restoration was doomed. But at this moment a
number of influential opponents of the dying regime became
alarmed at the magnitude of their own success. The wealthy men
of high finance, who bitterly resented the Restoration's
favouring of the clergy and the nobility, trembled at the prospect
of France recommencing the revolutionary adventure of 1789.
They certainly had no desire to see France become a republic. In
order to secure their position and to retain control of events they
lent support to the proposal that Louis-Philippe should accede
to the throne. A member of the Orleans family, Louis-Philippe
had served in the French army at Valmy and Jemmapes. Here
was a figure untainted by the sins of the Bourbons. On 31 July
Louis-Philippe was presented to the people of Paris by
Lafayette, the elderly hero of 1789. He was received with cheers
of acclamation by those assembled at the Hôtel de Ville. But
once safely established the July Monarchy offered little to those
ordinary Parisians who, by risking their lives on the barricades,

had brought the new regime into being. The monarch's personal power remained great. The franchise was not widened. Prudence was the order of the day as far as foreign policy was concerned. Those who had hoped for a republic felt sorely betrayed. Disillusionment increased. On obtaining positions of influence, Guizot and Cousin jettisoned their liberalism. Socially conservative, the July Monarchy struck many Frenchmen as egoistic, hypocritical, unprincipled and materialistic. Here was an acquisitive society with no sense of common purpose. In November 1831 a revolt by the silk-weavers of Lyons was brutally suppressed. Other industrial conflicts followed. Political agitation increased, culminating in April 1834 in the massacre of the Rue Transnonain when an attempted insurrection was put down by the National Guard. The government's resolve could not be doubted. One king had taken the place of another but the lot of the majority of citizens was unchanged. In the opinion of many the July Revolution had been betrayed, conjured away, 'escamotée'.

The similarities between the sequence of events just described and the plot of *Lorenzaccio* were remarked upon by the play's earliest commentators. Hippolyte Fortoul, reviewing the play in the pages of the *Revue des deux mondes*, observed: 'Ces marchands se laissent escamoter la république, à peu près aussi imprudemment qu'on l'a fait en ces temps derniers'.[2] Contemporary reference is indeed an essential aspect of *Lorenzaccio*. In his study *Musset et le théâtre intérieur*, Bernard Masson distinguishes three main areas of reference to the France of the July Monarchy (*31*, pp.32-35). Firstly, there is anti-clericalism which was a prominent feature in the political debate of the 1830s. Secondly, the theme of tyrannicide: an attempt was made on Louis-Philippe's life in 1832 and it was felt that the monarch's life, like that of Alexandre, was in permanent danger. Thirdly, we must not forget that *Lorenzaccio* is concerned with a revolt directed against a foreign occupying force and that in the wake of the July Revolution a rebellion had taken place in Italy against the Austrian military presence. There was in fact much in the play which struck a chord

[2] *Revue des deux mondes* 3e série, III (Sept. 1834), 610.

in the contemporary reader. Republicans in *Lorenzaccio* are recognised by the cut of their beards — a feature of 1830. Balls and masquerades were as popular in Musset's Paris as in Lorenzo's Florence. The Goldsmith's remark after the failure of the attempted rising — 'Les étudiants seuls se sont montrés' (V, 5, 3536-37) — recalls the devotion to the revolutionary cause shown by the 'jeunesse des écoles'. And Niccolini's fear that the ruling class will be overthrown was familiar to many of Musset's contemporaries: 'Si nous n'avons pas un duc ce soir ou demain, c'en est fait de nous. Le peuple est en ce moment comme l'eau qui va bouillir' (V, 1, 3272-73). But it is in his treatment of the opposition that Musset makes his greatest impact. Had not recent events taught that too many Frenchmen were, like Bindo Altoviti, willing to sacrifice their principles for personal advancement? Philippe himself is a recognisable type in the political context of the 1830s. His admiration for ancient Rome recalls the republican tradition of the French Revolution, obsessed with classical models. Moreover, by contrasting Lorenzo's political views with those of Philippe, Musset is pointing to the contradictions, to the lack of coherence within contemporary republicanism. Philippe, as I have already indicated, is seeking to restore the power of the old Florentine nobility. Lorenzo sees things differently. He believes that republican success rests upon the need to unite a much broader opposition movement including the ordinary people of Florence: 'Qu'ils [les républicains] aient pour eux le peuple, et tout est dit' (III, 3, 2194-95). These two strands of republicanism would have been well known to the reading public of the 1830s. There is a further point, however. This concerns the final scene of the play where Côme, the new Duke, swears on the Bible that he will serve the causes of freedom and justice. What is interesting is that in writing this scene Musset modified his historical sources in a significant manner. Joyce Bromfield, in her study *De Lorenzino de Médicis à 'Lorenzaccio'* (*20*), analyses the changes concerning the last act. She writes that in Varchi's *Storia Fiorentina* the murder takes place on a Saturday evening. The following morning, amid general confusion, the Cardinal warns the military commanders. The body of the Duke is discovered on

Sunday evening. The next morning the Cardinal is still uncertain of being able to control events but the arrival of Côme on the Monday evening saves him. The election of the new Duke takes place on Tuesday morning. Musset alters and compresses this material in order to reveal the Cardinal's skill in manipulating the Council of Eight. But by so doing he also emphasises the parallels with 1830. We are shown how easily the people are duped: 'Pauvre peuple! quel badaud on fait de toi!' (V, 1, 3312). A most apposite remark. In the final scene Musset departs significantly from Varchi's narrative. This is the moment when the newly elected Côme delivers his speech in the main square of Florence. The stage directions set the scene: *'Florence. — La grande place. Des tribunes publiques sont remplies de monde. Des gens du peuple accourent de tous côtés'* (V, 7). Now Bromfield tells us that according to Varchi the speech was not given in public at all (*20*, p.167). By changing the setting Musset could not fail to evoke memories of the moment when Louis-Philippe appeared with Lafayette on the balcony of the Hôtel de Ville. One monarch replaces another, one Duke replaces another. Nothing is changed. The 'garçon boucher' has been succeeded by 'un planteur de choux' (I, 2, 194; V, 6, 3628).

There remains, however, the delicate question of the nature of Musset's own political views. For we must not forget that Musset, the ironist, the dandy, professed a general indifference to social and political matters. Not for him the Hugolian stance of the poet-prophet guiding his fellow men to a better future. He preferred to pour scorn on the optimistic, progressive strain in Romantic thought. Politics and literature did not mix: 'si la littérature veut exister, il faut qu'elle rompe en visière à la politique'.[3] But Musset was not indifferent to politics and as a young man he showed clear liberal sympathies (see *22*). Claude Duchet remarks that at least until July 1830 Musset considered himself 'comme un jeune libéral, avec une certaine distance ironique, qui était sa façon d'être adolescent, et poète' (*7*, p.103). In fact Musset remained deeply aware of the socio-political dimension of human experience. His quest for authenticity was grounded in social reality. He was acutely

[3] *Œuvres complètes en prose* (Paris, Gallimard, 1960), p.761.

conscious that the crises which mark the life of the individual
contain a collective dimension. His novel, *La Confession d'un
enfant du siècle* (1836), makes just this point. It tells of a young
man's attempt to construct a substitute religion of human love.
The details of the story need not concern us here. What is
important is Musset's contention that the spiritual malady from
which his hero is suffering has causes which are social, political
and historical in nature: 'Toute la maladie du siècle présent vient
de deux causes; le peuple qui a passé par 93 et par 1814 porte au
cœur deux blessures. Tout ce qui était n'est plus; tout ce qui sera
n'est pas encore. Ne cherchez pas ailleurs le secret de nos
maux'.[4]

Alienated from society, stranded in the present, Musset's
contemporaries felt frustrated and dissatisfied. Moral and
spiritual life resembled a feverish sterility. Many turned their
attention to the past. At a time of crisis when old institutions
were breaking down, when systems of belief and thought were
giving way, the writers and thinkers of the nineteenth century
endeavoured to demonstrate that human history possessed a
hidden order. A vast array of philosophies of history was
elaborated in order to take account of historical change, to
relate the adventure of man's history to the cosmic drama.
History, it was felt, was less the work of individuals than of
ideas or of forces which underlay and explained the pattern of
events. Most agreed that history had a purpose although they
often disagreed as to what that purpose was. Change was the
governing principle of human existence, collective and
individual; but change was not random, it was a process of
becoming, of development, the unfolding of purpose.
Individuals and social groups alike were viewed as agents and
the movement of world history was regarded as progressive in
character.

But this passionate concern for the past did not just produce
grandiose interpretations and general theories. It inspired such
cultural phenomena as the fascination for the Gothic Middle
Ages and the interest in the civilisations of the ancient East. It
was also largely responsible for the development of Romantic

[4] *La Confession d'un enfant du siècle* (Paris, Gallimard, 1973), 36.

historical drama. Drama was the form which best conveyed the reality of historical experience. Frank Paul Bowman writes that 'the Romantics felt that the forces which create society are multiple and complex, and the representation of this multiple complexity could best be accomplished in the dramatic form' (*1*, p.122). During the 1820s writers attempted to capture the texture, the feeling of history in works comprising a number of rapidly changing short scenes. The most celebrated example of this dramatic form was Vitet's *Les Barricades* (1826). It was after the manner of works such as this that George Sand composed her *Une Conspiration en 1537* to which I referred in my introductory note. The prime aim of the 'scène historique' was fidelity. On this Vitet was adamant. In his introduction to *Les Barricades* he denied that he had written a drama at all: 'Ce n'est point une pièce de théâtre que l'on va lire, ce sont des faits historiques présentés sous la forme dramatique, mais sans la prétention d'en composer un drame'.[5] Such works were intended for reading rather than performance. What counted was truth to history. Musset follows in this tradition. In *Lorenzaccio* he transports us from street to palace, from Florence to Venice. He guides us through the different strata of Florentine society. We see the merchants selling their goods, the courtiers at play, the republicans plotting. The characters live and influence the action but they are also representative types. Musset recreates small but telling aspects of social reality: soldiers in the streets or young students struggling to catch sight of the rich and famous. By using so many characters the dramatist can project a wider vision of Florentine society, a vision which allows for a variation of viewpoint and a shifting of emphasis. To quote Frank Paul Bowman once again: 'Romantics often concluded that the ambiguities of life, or of any problem, can never be resolved, and authors found in the drama a form which would permit a simultaneous statement of these ambiguities' (*1*, p.122).

There is, however, a vast difference between the scrupulous reproduction of historical reality as practised by Vitet and the broad sweep of Musset's imaginative vision. Musset does not

[5] *Les Barricades* (Paris, Renouard, 1827), V.

let himself be too constrained by his subject matter. The dramatist's intention is to write a tightly organised play and he feels under no obligation to follow Varchi's *Storia Fiorentina* to the letter. He takes considerable liberties with chronology. It was no secret to Musset that the historical Lorenzo was killed more than a decade after the murder of Alexandre. Similarly he was well aware that Nasi's ball took place during the winter of 1532-33 and that Louise Strozzi was poisoned in December 1534 (*31*, p.89). Musset chose deliberately to modify the order of events. A parallel lack of respect for historical reality emerges when we look at the process of the creation of character. The real Philippe Strozzi was cynical and worldly-wise. Musset's Philippe is quite different. Only a noble, upright but naïve Philippe could plausibly provoke the younger man into unburdening his soul in Act Three. But Musset goes further than this. Varchi mentions a liaison between Ricciarda and Alexandre but says nothing of her character. The development of the sub-plot is Musset's invention (*20*, p.150).

Musset absorbs, modifies and reworks the historical data provided by Varchi and already put to good use by George Sand in *Une Conspiration en 1537*. He aims at truthfulness and realism in the spirit of the 'scène historique' whilst at the same time making indirect comments on recent political events in France. In addition he draws upon his own experience in order to lay bare the contradictions of human nature. It is time now to consider a further important question. Does *Lorenzaccio* present us with a coherent view of the nature of historical change?

Is history a progressive movement whose course men can understand and influence? Or is history an impersonal force possessed of its own momentum? One way of approaching these problems is to ask what changes actually take place in the course of the play. An examination of the final scenes suggests that nothing of substance has changed at all. The Goldsmith still laments the state of Florence. The Strozzi still hate the Salviati as the squabble between the two schoolboys admirably illustrates. Even Ricciarda Cibo has returned to the arms of her husband. The Duke has been killed but a new Duke has been elected. Tyranny has been reimposed and life continues as before. The soldiers keep order and the people, acquiescing in their servitude, acclaim the election of Côme. The only significant change would appear to be a further strengthening of the Cardinal's hand. He has succeeded in preventing revolution and imposed his chosen candidate as Duke. Côme will be a more pliant instrument of the Cardinal than Alexandre was. Evil triumphs in the ironic final scene in which Côme solemnly swears to God (and to the Cardinal!) that he will uphold the cause of justice.

Lorenzo correctly predicted that nothing would change as a result of his killing the Duke. His attempts to warn the republicans were dismissed as the ramblings of a drunken prankster. In the event, distributions of wine and food suffice to rescue the established order from the dangers which threaten it. The people are incapable of becoming genuine actors on the stage of history and allow themselves to be relegated to the status of spectators. For the election of Côme cannot be attributed solely to the Cardinal's skill in directing affairs. Even when chance seems to favour the cause of change, human nature conspires against it. The reaction of the republicans to Corsini's offer to hand over the fortress is exemplary: 'on a braillé, bu du vin sucré, et cassé des carreaux; mais la proposition de ce brave homme n'a seulement pas été écoutée. Comme on n'osait pas faire ce qu'il voulait, on a dit qu'on doutait de lui, et qu'on le soupçonnait de fausseté dans ses offres' (V, 5, 3546-50). Mankind appears to be incapable, unwilling to transform its condition. No co-ordination of effort can compensate for human limitations and open up the way to improvement.

Musset's characters entertain different relationships with history (*34*). The Duke, whose sole aim is sensual gratification, has no concern to decipher the meaning of history. The future of Florence is of no interest to him. Philippe Strozzi, for his part, perceives the present in relation to his idealised vision of the Florentine and Classical past. He remains outside the movement of history until events compel his participation. Lorenzo too stands outside history and cannot really be viewed as fulfilling the destiny of a revolutionary hero. His motives are ultimately personal, not political, and he has no sense of acting in accordance with the general direction of history. As he later remarks to Philippe: 'Je ne nie pas l'histoire, mais je n'y étais pas' (V, 2, 3422). Can any stable meaning be assigned to the passing of time? Or are all attempts at explanation really just as futile, just as unworthy of serious consideration, as the Silk Merchant's 'combinaisons surnaturelles' based upon the mystical significance of the number six (V, 5, 3505)?

Is time in fact an illusion? In an important article, 'L'Esthétique de *Lorenzaccio*', Hassan El Nouty has argued that the movement of the play is best seen as a return of sameness. History is repetition without meaning. The murder was a chaotic disturbance, a disruption of history but it achieved nothing at all. Musset's understanding of history is therefore darkly pessimistic. No remedy can avail against the flux of time which brings decay and dissolution. El Nouty draws a useful comparison between *Lorenzaccio* and Michelet's *Introduction à l'histoire universelle* (1831). Jules Michelet, the great historian of the French Revolution, interpreted world history as a vast movement towards greater freedom. Inspired by the events of July 1830 Michelet saw in the French nation the concrete embodiment of mankind's aspiration to liberty. Musset lacked Michelet's confidence in man and his faith in history. But whilst he was disinclined to view history in terms of the progressive self-realisation of a higher purpose, he remained very conscious of the reality of historical change. Therein, according to El Nouty, lies the force of Musset's drama: 'L'originalité de *Lorenzaccio* c'est précisément de préserver la notion de devenir tout en la vidant du contenu providentiel ou mythique qu'y introduit un anthropocentrisme tenace' (*24*, p.602).

Musset is saying something very interesting. A witness to his age and its mental dispositions, he brings a whole society before us. He articulates opinions and points of view which might otherwise have been left unexpressed. This approach is in fact reminiscent of Michelet's concern for the multifarious aspects of social life. Musset, however, does not organise experience in order to point to the unfolding of purpose: history manifests no sign of the existence of an ordering presence. Whereas other

Romantics embarked upon a quest for harmony and unity, a search for an order which they felt lay hidden beneath the appearances of nature and history, the main thrust of *Lorenzaccio* is to show the futility of such aspirations. Nature is not really a source of solace and history is no more a home, no more a habitable space than Florence. History has no soul, and the individual subject is incapable of generating meaning. Men are neither ends in themselves nor means to attain ends which transcend them. The displacement of politics into literature reveals a pattern of sameness, of repetition. There is no mediation of the ideal, no delivrance. Lorenzo feels nostalgia for childhood, for purity, but he experiences no clear urge towards repentance. Morality has lost its foundations. The human mind cannot be knit to the passing of time. In contrast to those who saw history as a reservoir of energy, a realm of possibility, a ground of value, Musset seems to be saying that neither freedom nor reconciliation is realisable. History cannot be taken as proof of the existence of a divine order. Temporal change is the condition of all things but if change has a meaning it is corruption, surrender, decay. The real tragedy of *Lorenzaccio* is the collective tragedy of belief, of hope.

In *Lorenzaccio*, therefore, Musset has successfully fused a meditation on contemporary political reality with a recreation of the Florentine past. At the same time he has made a statement of general import concerning the tragedy of the human condition conceived in historical terms. His vision transcends his age. Yet whilst achieving that which many of his contemporaries failed to attain — an adequate representation of a society's experience in dramatic form — Musset does so in order to call into question the very notion of history as progress and development. In his play history defies all attempts at control: even the Cardinal cannot prevent the Duke's assassination and the risk of revolution. For Musset there could be neither acceptance of imperfection nor transcendence of human limitations. Like Lorenzo, he knew and felt himself to be isolated. *Lorenzaccio* marked a meeting with history, an encounter which was at once an acknowledgment of the historicity of all things and a recognition of the absence of meaning. There is no better

52 *Lorenzaccio*

description of Musset's complex relation to history than that
provided by Max Milner: 'le sujet de *Lorenzaccio* offrait le seul
biais par lequel Musset pût, à travers son histoire, rejoindre
l'Histoire — ou plus exactement s'en désolidariser avec mépris'
(*4*, p.218).

4 The Mask and the Word

The central organising image of *Lorenzaccio* is that of the mask. The mask disguises. It creates uncertainty. It facilitates the practice of deceit, encourages the will to power whilst simultaneously inviting unmasking, issuing a challenge to others to respond to its illusion of presence. Musset's imagination transforms the mask into a rich and ambiguous metaphor. Instead of veiling the solid substance of reality the mask takes on a life of its own, testifying to the inescapable instability of all things. Life, Musset seems to be saying, is a masquerade, a spectacle, a form of theatre. This impression is successfully conveyed in Act One. First there is the Silk Merchant's reference to Carnival, to that moment of temporary excess and confusion of roles. Then we join the spectators watching the guests as they depart from the masked ball. This scene is not included simply to convey background information: it fulfils a far more important function. It allows Musset to open up a literary space in which the inversion of values will dominate, in which disguise will become an essential means of achieving one's ends. The notion of spectacle occurs again later in the same act in the scene which depicts the crowds leaving the church of Saint-Miniato at Montolivet. This is no religious pilgrimage. It is an occasion for the expression of vanity: 'Comme il a bien prêché! c'est le confesseur de ma fille' (I, 5, 546-47). It is an opportunity for the ladies of the nobility to purchase the silks and the articles of clothing which take their fancy. The ladies indulge in amorous intrigues and flirt with officers of the German garrison: 'Il est bête à faire plaisir, ton officier; que peux-tu faire de cela?' (I, 5, 606-07). Talk of republican resistance and patriotism contrasts starkly with the frivolity, the superficiality of the spectacle.

In the first instance the mask is designed to conceal. Such had been Lorenzo's intention. The mask would further his plan and at the same time protect his essence. The exterior would defend the interior; appearance would be the guardian of reality. In fact interiority disappears as Lorenzo becomes his mask. There is no longer an inside and an outside, no longer a 'liqueur précieuse' contained within a 'flacon' (III, 3, 1969-70). He admits to having really become a debauchee. He now accepts the name of Lorenzaccio, speaking his own condition in accordance with the judgment which society places on him. The mask, the exterior, is now the true, the real. But having assumed his own mask, Lorenzo acquires the capacity to see through the masks of others: 'tous les masques tombaient devant mon regard' (III, 3, 2130). Once we pass through the confusing veil of appearances, once the mask has ceased to obstruct our gaze, we encounter the omnipresence of evil and corruption. Thus Lorenzo detects the budding courtesan in Maffio's innocent sister. The surface of the ocean may appear calm and serene but beneath lie death and the Leviathan. To express the horror he felt at making this discovery Lorenzo employs a telling image: 'l'Humanité souleva sa robe, et me montra, comme à un adepte digne d'elle, sa monstrueuse nudité' (III, 3, 2130-32). Once this revelation had been vouchsafed it could never be forgotten. Nudity has the power to disconcert: the reader recalls Tebaldeo's reaction to Lorenzo's wish to commission the portrait of a naked courtesan. Clothing, on the other hand, partakes of the nature of the mask: 'Le vice a été pour moi un vêtement, maintenant il est collé à ma peau' (III, 3, 2174-75). The comparison comes easily to Lorenzo: 'Quand j'ai commencé à jouer mon rôle de Brutus moderne, je marchais dans mes habits neufs de la grande confrérie du vice, comme un enfant de dix ans dans l'armure d'un géant de la fable' (III, 3, 2122-25). Here is a further example:

Quel bourbier doit donc être l'espèce humaine, qui se rue ainsi dans les tavernes avec des lèvres affamées de débauche, quand moi, qui n'ai voulu prendre qu'un masque pareil à leurs visages, et qui ai été aux mauvais lieux avec une résolution inébranlable de rester pur sous mes vêtements souillés, je ne puis ni me retrouver moi-même, ni laver mes mains, même avec du sang! (IV, 5, 2897-903).

References to clothing abound in *Lorenzaccio* and it would be unwise to regard them as being of only secondary importance. Clothes fascinate: the young students crane their necks to catch a glimpse of the guests 'avec leurs habits de toutes les couleurs' (I, 2, 94-95). Clothes are at once a source and a symbol of wealth. This the Silk Merchant knows well: 'ce sont mes étoffes qui dansent, mes belles étoffes du bon Dieu, sur le cher corps de tous ces braves et loyaux seigneurs' (I, 2, 121-23). The vestimentary discourse underlines the view of life as a game, a dance, an expenditure of energy in the pursuit of pleasure. But not all who wish to go to the ball can do so. They are cast in the role of spectators.

In *Lorenzaccio* the opposition between appearance and reality is explored in terms of the relationship between the human body and the clothes which cover it. The body is perceived as the location of truth. For this reason the removal of clothing, the revealing of what lies beneath can be interpreted as an initiatory experience. Clothes are carriers of meaning, so many signs which mark the body which they simultaneously adorn and conceal. Musset's hero seeks to gain access to the authenticity which he feels resides in the body. A work written in a different spirit to that which informs *Lorenzaccio* might well have presented sexual love for a woman as a solution for Lorenzo's dilemma. The experience of physical union with the beloved might have signalled his release from isolation and inner division. In *Lorenzaccio*, however, knowledge of and fusion with the other involves the act of murder, the physical penetration of the body of Alexandre by violent means: '[le cœur d'Alexandre] est maintenant à nu sous ma main; je n'ai qu'à laisser tomber mon stylet pour qu'il y entre' (III, 3, 2058-60). In my discussion of the murder I emphasised the sexual connotations. I also drew attention to Lorenzo's desire not just to kill the Duke but to butcher, consume and appropriate the body, the truth of the other. Both of these elements are of relevance to our present concerns. For has not the body itself a surface, an inside and an outside? The 'corps à corps' is not enough to satisfy Lorenzo who needs to plunge his blade deeply into Alexandre's body as if to extract from it an ultimate meaning (III, 3, 2032). But is there any ultimate meaning? The violent search for truth leads inevitably to death. Lorenzo disappears beneath the waters of the lagoon. The body of the Duke is removed ignominiously, wrapped in a carpet (see *21*).

Closely associated with the theme of the mask is that of the dream. 'Le rêve' is a key word in *Lorenzaccio*, both in the usual meaning of dream (including nightmare and hallucination) and in the extended sense of hope or aspiration. Every character of significance in the play nurtures a particular dream. The 'rêve' is a mental construct, the embodiment of a wish, the formulation of an ideal. Marie dreamt of greatness for the son who seemed destined to 'couronner d'un diadème d'or tous [ses] songes chéris' (I, 6, 728-29). Philippe is unashamedly a dreamer, obsessed with hopes for mankind. Tebaldeo offers an aesthetic variation: 'Réaliser des rêves, voilà la vie du peintre' (II, 2, 919). Ricciarda Cibo has her dream of transforming the Duke by becoming his mistress. The Cardinal's dreams of power are boundless and he, moreover, tries to exploit his sister-in-law: 'J'étais sûr que vous commenceriez par vos rêves; il faudra cependant que vous en veniez quelque jour aux miens' (IV, 4, 2792-93). The Cardinal's dreams may yet become a reality but for the other characters to dream, to hope, is ultimately as pointless as to act. Dreams have the power to govern human lives but like masks they possess no genuine reality. In retrospect it would have been better if the dream had never been. As Marie remarks to Catherine: 'Ah! Cattina, pour dormir tranquille, il faut n'avoir jamais fait certains rêves' (I, 6, 730-31).

Yet such is the paradoxical nature of Musset's inverted world that the dreams which we experience in sleep are not dismissed as mere illusion. On the contrary. In the very first scene Maffio is awakened from his slumbers only to find his dream confirmed by reality. He steps into the garden still pondering the highly disturbing content of his dream: 'Il me semblait dans mon rêve voir ma sœur traverser notre jardin, tenant une lanterne sourde, et couverte de pierreries. Je me suis éveillé en sursaut. Dieu sait que ce n'est qu'une illusion, mais une illusion trop forte pour que le sommeil ne s'enfuie pas devant elle' (I, 1, 38-42).

Immediately, however, these premonitions are confirmed as Gabrielle crosses the garden precisely as foreseen in the dream. But in a deeper sense too dreams are capable of communicating truth. The obvious example is Marie's hallucinatory waking dream of Lorenzo's spectre to which I referred earlier. In this manner Musset leaves the reader unsure about the status of illusion and reality and the nature of their relation.

Musset's characters inhabit a world of uncertainty and danger, a world of appearances and surfaces. It is above all a world of masks. What could be more appropriate than the excuse which the Cardinal invokes to explain the Duke's absence from court on the morning following the murder: 'Le duc a passé la nuit à une mascarade, et il repose en ce moment' (VI, 1, 3263-64). Life is a spectacle, a shifting pattern of dreams and masks and this instability points to the underlying absence of moral certitudes. Language echoes this ambiguity. For as Lorenzo remarks to Valori: 'ce que vous dites là est parfaitement vrai et parfaitement faux, comme tout au monde' (II, 2, 883-84). Language, as I shall endeavour to show, is not to be trusted. It partakes of the same instability and ambiguity as the mask, and, like the mask, it can become an instrument of power, both seductive and dangerous, bestowing the illusion of reality and the simulacrum of presence.

In Musset's play words are a substitute for action. Speaking replaces doing. Words proliferate and disguise the failure to act. Lorenzo is left feeling exasperated: 'Ah! les mots, les mots, les éternelles paroles! ... O bavardage humain! ô grand tueur de corps morts! grand défonceur de portes ouvertes! ô hommes sans bras!' (IV, 9, 3068-72). Words proliferate and give the illusion of purposefully directed activity. Such is the essential weakness of the republicans and of Philippe Strozzi in particular. This 'inexorable faiseur de sentences' confuses the eloquent expression of political and philosophical conviction with the taking of action (IV, 6, 2976). He is in love with words and their supposed power: 'la république, il nous faut ce mot-là. Et quand ce ne serait qu'un mot, c'est quelque chose, puisque les peuples se lèvent quand il traverse l'air' (II, 1, 819-22). Instead of acting Philippe cries 'Agissons!' until the moment of crisis begins to recede (II, 5, 1466). It is as if repetition magically removed the consequences of the expression of intentionality. Hence Pierre's genuine failure to understand why his father is reluctant to join in the revolt: 'Ne vous ai-je pas entendu cent fois dire ce que nous disons?' (III, 3, 1751-52). Pierre has not grasped that for his father language has become an alibi, a method of warding off all unpleasant contact with reality. Words do not facilitate contact with the world. Instead they become dissociated from the objects which they are intended to designate.

The republicans are hollow men, and their appeal to patriotism and the good of mankind is without real foundation. The energies of the opposition are dissipated in empty rhetoric. Lorenzo has learnt this from experience: 'j'ai bu, dans les banquets patriotiques, le vin qui engendre la métaphore et la prosopopée' (III, 3, 2141-42). The practitioners of wordy eloquence take a self-conscious delight in their speech-making. Language becomes a toy to play with, an instrument of personal vanity. Lorenzo makes this plain to Venturi and Bindo Altoviti:

> Vous ne connaissez pas la véritable éloquence. On tourne une grande période autour d'un beau petit mot, pas trop court ni trop long, et rond comme une toupie. On rejette son bras gauche en arrière de manière à faire faire à son manteau des plis pleins d'une dignité tempérée par la grâce; on lâche sa période qui se déroule comme une corde ronflante, et la petite toupie s'échappe avec un murmure délicieux. On pourrait presque la ramasser dans le creux de la main, comme les enfants des rues (II, 4, 1271-79).

Eloquence of the kind mocked by Lorenzo in these lines recalls the bad poetry of the absurd tutor who sings the praises of liberty in the last act.

But need words be the enemy of action? Must they conceal rather than reveal reality? Claude Duchet reminds us that Ricciarda, Philippe, Maffio and Tebaldeo all 'croient, un moment tout au moins, à une efficacité, à une vertu de la parole' (*23*, p.151). The belief persists that language can reproduce reality and communicate experience. Language, it is felt, is a transparent medium which allows the accurate reporting of what has taken place. 'Dis les choses comme elles sont' cries Pierre to Léon Strozzi as he tries to find out about the insult (II, 1, 857). For Ricciarda Cibo the belief persists that there exists a direct correspondence between words and things, between language and the world: '[les] mots représentent des pensées, et ces pensées des actions' (I, 3, 340-41). Language creates inter-subjectivity and a recognition of community of attitude. As Tebaldeo says to Valori: 'Trouver sur les lèvres d'un honnête homme ce qu'on a soi-même dans le cœur, c'est le plus grand des bonheurs qu'on puisse désirer' (II, 2, 889-91). Language — or so it seems — can also form a unifying bond between the self and the world of nature. There is the example of the 'harangue sentimentale' which the Marquis delivers on his wife's behalf to her beloved countryside (I, 3, 289). Finally, language gives access to a transcendent realm of value to which reference can be made. When we first encounter Maffio in the garden he appeals to justice and refuses to die in silence. The reality of the ideal of justice is not questioned. It is proclaimed in adversity.

Yet the whole movement of *Lorenzaccio* suggests that there is no realm of value to which we gain entry through language. Justice is a mere word. Freedom likewise. We cannot transform the conditions of existence by invoking concepts which have no reality outside language. Words do not knit directly to the objects they name. Speech does not reinstate value. As Maffio discovers that the Duke to whose justice he is appealing is in fact the very man who is abducting his sister so Ricciarda discovers to her cost that her verbal expression of political idealism was in fact a displacement of desire. Such contradictions add to the ironic tone of the play. The Cardinal's perceptive mind seizes upon the difference between what he hears and what he sees: 'Cela est comique d'entendre les fureurs de cette pauvre marquise, et de la voir courir à un rendez-vous d'amour avec le cher tyran, toute baignée de larmes républicaines' (I, 3, 366-69). Indeed the Cardinal succeeds because there exists no ideal truth of which our notion of truth expressed in and through language is a reflexion. Words do not, indeed cannot, have a fixed meaning. Everything is simultaneously both true and false. Those who, in Ricciarda's words 'mettent les mots sur leur enclume, et qui les tordent avec un marteau et une lime', know that language is malleable (I, 3, 338-40). Words are objects, instruments of the will to power, so much currency to be used to the greatest effect. Language does not convey objective truth. It is organised in accordance with the strategy of the user.

When viewed in this light words retain their essential power. The central case in point is obviously the insult. Salviati's words to Louise Strozzi and the remarks subsequently addressed to Léon Strozzi cannot be ignored. Their force is such that they command a response from the Strozzi whose collective sense of honour has been grievously offended. A few words are sufficient to set events in train for these are words which impinge directly upon the world of action: 'Un propos! ... voilà les guerres de famille, voilà comme les couteaux se tirent' (II, 5, 1373-75). Here we are not dealing with eloquence, with the gaudy play of language which serves to embroider the clichés of political discourse. The insult is a weapon: 'ils savent bien où ils frappent' (II, 5, 1401-02). Words can contain a destructive charge as we see from Marie Soderini's reactions after Catherine has read her the letter she has received from the Duke: 'J'ai trop souffert, ma pauvre Catherine; pourquoi m'as-tu lu cette lettre? je ne puis plus rien supporter' (III, 4, 2295-97). Marie finds in the Duke's letter the confirmation of her worst fears concerning her son's conduct. She is left feeling that her end is near.

It would seem, therefore, that whilst words have lost their anchorage in the ontological order they retain the power to influence the course of human destiny. Lorenzo's long speech in the opening scene invites us to reflect upon the manner in which language can be used to achieve the desired effect: 'infiltrer paternellement le filon mystérieux du vice dans un conseil d'ami, dans une caresse au menton — tout dire et ne rien dire, selon le caractère des parents' (I, 1, 14-16). The crucial difference lies between what words say and what they mean. What matters is to achieve the correct response. Lorenzo appears to enjoy the power which his control of language affords him. He provokes Sire Maurice, plays with Tebaldeo, ridicules Venturi and Bindo

Altoviti. There appear to be no limits to the power of language to corrupt the innocent: 'Catherine n'est-elle pas vertueuse, irréprochable? Combien faudrait-il pourtant de paroles pour faire de cette colombe ignorante la proie de ce gladiateur aux poils roux? Quand je pense que j'ai failli parler!' (V, 4, 2908-11).

Lorenzo is painfully aware of the gap between word and deed. He feels exasperated, conscious as he is of the futility of all the 'bavardage' which is going on about him. Yet for all this he remains caught, trapped within the web of language. In his long scene with Philippe is he perhaps a trifle too eloquent? Lorenzo longs for a lost wholeness, for the innocence which was once his at Cafaggiuolo. His aim is to overcome disunity through action. But even here he cannot escape language which binds him irrevocably to the world of inauthenticity and corruption. Indeed, before he kills Alexandre, Lorenzo has already defined his act in terms which acknowledge that the murder will have no practical consequences. An excellent formulation by W. Moser sums up the attitude of the main protagonist: '[Lorenzo] achève la dépréciation anticipée de son faire en le réduisant à un dire et à une écriture' (*33*, p.101). The passage in question reads as follows:

> Que les hommes me comprennent ou non, qu'ils agissent ou n'agissent pas, j'aurai dit tout ce que j'ai à dire; je leur ferai tailler leurs plumes, si je ne leur fais pas nettoyer leurs piques, et l'Humanité gardera sur sa joue le soufflet de mon épée marqué en traits de sang. (III, 3, 2247-52)

We can now grasp fully the apposite nature of Moser's remarks. Lorenzo, looking to the future, regards the murder not as a revolutionary act but as a way of at last having his say, of gaining revenge on those who despise him, of obliging men to record his name in their collective memory.

The Duke, on the other hand, shows little interest in language. He does not respond to Lorenzo's long speech in the first scene. His mind is firmly set on obtaining the young Gabrielle, the object of his desire. We have already seen how he finds Ricciarda Cibo's political speeches tedious and quite simply

superfluous: 'Des mots, des mots, et rien de plus' (III, 6, 2326).
Awaiting the arrival of Catherine Ginori he once again makes
plain that he seeks physical pleasure alone. Hence his remark to
Lorenzo: 'Tu sais que je n'aime pas les bavardages, et il m'est
revenu que la Catherine était une belle parleuse. Pour éviter les
conversations, je vais me mettre au lit' (IV, 11, 3178-80). The
Duke's language corresponds to his personality: his colourful
speech is peppered with oaths such as 'entrailles du diable' (II, 4,
1334). Neither expansive in conversation, nor fulsome in his
letters, Alexandre is not given to use language in novel ways. His
life of debauchery is in fact a life of action. But we must not be
misled here. Alexandre is undoubtedly coarse, vulgar and direct,
quite lacking in Lorenzo's verbal skills, and yet he knows that if
he so desires his words have the power to transform people's
lives completely. He may decide to have Maffio banished and
Pierre and Thomas Strozzi arrested. On the one hand we have
the fervent but vacuous declarations of a Philippe Strozzi. On
the other we have the Duke whose rule is arbitrary but whose
word is law. What need has Alexandre of the persuasive powers
of eloquence: 'Qui parle ici, quand je parle?' (I, 5, 514).

The question of the nature and function of language lies at the
heart of Musset's creation. His characters are themselves
perplexed by language, by its fluidity, and by its capacity
simultaneously to conceal and reveal. The scenes involving the
Cardinal are interesting from this point of view. In the first place
we see the Cardinal as a man eager to use language as a tool of
domination. In dealing with his sister-in-law he is usually adept
in obtaining the reactions he seeks although there are moments
when he appears to be somewhat reckless in what he advances.
The key scene is of course the confessional. The Cardinal
interrogates Ricciarda. He tries to make her divulge the name of
the sender of the letter. She resists this: 'Lire une lettre peut être
un péché, mais non pas lire une signature. Qu'importe le nom à
la chose?' (II, 3, 1114-15). In fact the Cardinal already knows
that the author was the Duke. But he also knows that his
interests will only really be served by having Ricciarda
pronounce the name of the Duke. The verbal admission is all-
important since from the moment of utterance the name of the

Duke ceases to be Ricciarda's secret and becomes the sign of the Cardinal's power over her. Yet while the Cardinal shows his verbal skills in his relations with his sister-in-law he behaves in a significantly different manner in the wider political context. Here silence, not language, is the key to success. His role is to act 'sans parler', in accordance with the orders he has received from the Vatican (II, 3, 1035). No one knows better than the Cardinal that power is not synonymous with the trappings of power. His intention is to direct events in a relatively unobtrusive manner, to use language sparingly but to good effect. His conduct in the chaotic circumstances which follow the assassination is particularly illuminating. Panic reigns at the ducal palace. The Cardinal is not present on stage even though the survival of the established order depends upon the efficacy of the steps which he is taking. He makes a brief entrance (V, 1, 3261) but when asked what has been decided he replies with a Latin quotation from Virgil. The Cardinal knows that at this juncture speech-making will not assure the maintenance of the status quo. Decisive but discreet action is required. There is a striking contrast between the conduct of the Cardinal and the behaviour of the other characters who appear before us. Florence is full of sound, of noise. We hear the courtiers express their fears as the 'vacarme' of the people swells threateningly in the streets (V, 5, 3525). We hear the mystical ramblings of the Silk Merchant and the absurd verses of the writer of sonnets. The moment of crisis produces words, more words and precious little action. The Cardinal is absent from the stage but he is busy silently organising the triumph of Côme. The Cardinal does not need to be elected to the dukedom in order to achieve his aims. He will govern through Côme. The final words of the play may safely be left to Côme, this 'beau dévideur de paroles', for his phrases are empty formulations, lacking in any real substance (V, 5, 3519). In this manner the concluding scene further emphasises the discrepancy between words and things. It is the existence of this gap which allows the Cardinal to succeed. But, as we have seen, the whole movement of the play calls into question the capacity of language to describe, reflect or transform human experience. In some instances words are dangerous because they distort our view of the world. In others, words take on more reality than life itself. Thus it is that the exiled supporters of Philippe fail to rally to the cause of his son Pierre. Only the name of Philippe Strozzi possesses the power to galvanise the opposition forces into action: 'Les confédérés veulent le nom de Philippe; nous ne ferons rien sans cela' (IV, 8, 3024-25).

At the start of the present chapter I remarked that the mask was the central organising metaphor in *Lorenzaccio*. My subsequent observations have suggested that Musset's pre-occupation with the mask merges with a more general reflection on the phenomenon of language which masks the world which it purports to represent. Words do not really assist the pursuit of meaning and all who desire authenticity are obliged to distrust language which is neither a repository of truth nor a way of solving life. The relation of the dramatist to language is therefore a precarious one since he is compelled to use this unstable medium in order to convey his essential intuition that a man's motives may be quite different from what he asserts. Language, like the mask, is of the order of the surface. But impatience with language does not render action any more successful. Man is left struggling to cope with the onrushing flow of time. The mask does not preserve reality. The word does not defend value. Life is diminished and man, conscious of his impotence, is unable to subdue the demands of unease.

5 Dramatic Coherence

I have already observed that *Lorenzaccio* was written to be read rather than performed. For a long time this was indeed its fate. Musset died in 1857 with his work remaining 'un spectacle dans un fauteuil'. An attempt to stage an adaptation of the play was made during the 1860s but the plan, perhaps predictably, fell foul of the imperial censor. Debauchery and political assassination were not considered subjects fit to be portrayed before the theatre-going public of the Second Empire. Only in 1896 was a version of *Lorenzaccio* performed, and on this occasion the role of Lorenzo was taken by the famous actress, Sarah Bernhardt. Subsequent productions (1926, 1927, 1945) also chose an actress to play the male lead. In retrospect the procedure must be considered a failure. An attempt to use a male actor was made at Bordeaux in 1933 but the practice only really became established in 1952 with the successful staging of the play by the Théâtre National Populaire (*17*, p.177). Gérard Philipe headed the cast. In recent years there have been two memorable productions. The first, by the Czech director Otomar Krejča, was brought to Paris in 1970. The second, by Franco Zeffirelli, was staged at the Comédie Française in 1976. All who are interested in the fascinating history of earlier productions of *Lorenzaccio* are recommended to consult the third section of Bernard Masson's exhaustive study *Musset et le théâtre intérieur*.

But why should *Lorenzaccio* have taken so long to reach the stage? Political considerations and worries concerning the play's morality certainly played their part but there were also problems of a more practical nature. How was a late nineteenth-century or early twentieth-century director to cope with thirty-eight scenes, with a cast of over forty players? The numerous changes of scene posed insuperable difficulties. The technical resources at the disposal of the director were inadequate to the task. Furthermore, with the fall from favour of Romantic historical drama *Lorenzaccio*'s chances of being successfully performed inevitably suffered. A play which epitomised the Romantic desire to emulate Shakespeare held no appeal for unconditional admirers of the classical ideal (see *17*, p.121). Was Musset's play a formless monster, a dangerous deviation from the traditions of seventeenth-century theatre?

Our estimate of the play is very different. Musset's meditation on the mobility of the personality and his sombre vision of society have struck a chord in audiences since the end of the Second World War. But it is not simply a matter of *Lorenzaccio* corresponding to the temper of modern times, to the concerns of a Europe which could not avoid engaging with the questions raised by Sartre's *Les Mains sales*. In recent years *Lorenzaccio* has been examined in detail and the significance of the play's dramatic structure has been reassessed. Its form has been analysed in relation to its controlling ideas, and critics, no longer taking simple regularity as their ideal, have come to realise that behind the apparent formlessness lies the search for a different dramatic form, for a form capable of expressing the collective truth of a society as well as the psychological truth of an individual. Discontinuity is not a synonym for incoherence. From being consigned for ever to the printed page, *Lorenzaccio* has become one of the few Romantic dramas considered worthy of performance (see *4*, p.218).

The absolute centrality of Lorenzo's destiny is beyond question. He dominates at least seventeen of the thirty-eight scenes. One fact, however, needs always to be borne in mind. We are not dealing with a play which builds up to a shattering moment of self-discovery. That discovery has been made by Lorenzo *before* the action actually begins. The point is rather that the true import of this discovery is only gradually revealed to the audience through the unfolding of events. The opening scene portrays Lorenzo as a cynical debauchee. This picture appears to be confirmed by what follows. Soon, nevertheless, Musset is signalling to his audience that all is not what it seems to be. 'C'est bien fort, c'est bien fort!' comments the Cardinal after Lorenzo has just fainted, thus alerting us to the possibility of ambiguity (I, 5, 539). At this stage no precise information is conveyed but gradually our doubts concerning Lorenzo's real motives are increased. Marie paints the picture of her son's idealistic youth. Is this man really a coward? A remark by Bindo Altoviti adds to our suspicions: 'Je t'ai vu faire des armes à Rome' (II, 4, 1243). Lorenzo's own enigmatic utterances help to mould our reactions: 'si mon spectre revient, dites-lui qu'il verra bientôt quelque chose qui l'étonnera' (II, 4, 1231-32). The removal of the Duke's chain-mail shirt prepares us directly for the assassination and at the start of Act Three Lorenzo openly declares to Scoronconcolo: 'Tu as deviné mon mal — j'ai un ennemi' (III, 1, 1673). Once this amount of information has been communicated, Musset can afford to allow Lorenzo to explain his motives to Philippe. The audience's attention has been held; suspense successfully created. In other words, in *Lorenzaccio* psychological revelation is intimately related to the working out of the plot. The conflicts and oppositions (Lorenzo/Alexandre, Lorenzo/Tebaldeo, Lorenzo/Philippe) serve both to generate events and to reveal psychological truth.

But given the central position occupied by Lorenzo we are inevitably led to enquire whether Musset develops the play's wider action in a satisfactory manner. At first sight the pattern of events may appear confusing and we may legitimately wonder whether our attention is being distracted by external or peripheral concerns. Robert Horville distinguishes no fewer than five strands of plot. These are associated with, respectively, Lorenzo, Ricciarda Cibo, Philippe Strozzi, Pierre Strozzi, and the Florentine people in general. Each is presented to the spectator, developed and carried through to its own conclusion. Is there not a danger that the sub-plots will lead us away from the predicament of the main protagonist and hinder the play's dramatic effectiveness? It has often been remarked that Ricciarda Cibo never comes into contact with either Lorenzo or Philippe. Initially this may suggest a failure of organisation on Musset's behalf and we may be tempted to view the scenes in which Ricciarda appears as somehow inessential. But to do so is to misconceive the play's real strength. Musset is not seeking to produce a continuous movement, a linear development. By making use of a number of different narrative elements he highlights the fundamental isolation of the characters who are unable to formulate a coherent revolutionary strategy. The very elements of discontinuity which are apparent to all readers, the sudden shifts from one plot-line to another, give further emphasis to the play's major moral concerns. Despite their irreducible isolation the characters with republican sympathies confront the same obstacle (the Duke) and resist the same hostile force (the Cardinal embodying the joint power of the Papacy and the Holy Roman Empire). They have in common a shared experience of the evils of Florentine society. Most of all they are all shown to be united in their ultimate failure (see *26*, pp.28-32).

We may now turn to the matter of the play's internal chronology. The reader of *Lorenzaccio* swiftly takes note of the numerous indications of time of day and time of year. Here are some examples, all drawn from Act One: '*Clair de lune*' (I, 1); 'Il fait un froid de tous les diables' (I, 1, 2); 'Mon portefeuille me glace les mains' (I, 2, 96); 'Le soleil commence à baisser' (I, 1, 670); '*Le soleil est couché*' (I, 6, 755). Such evidence allows us to perceive the temporal movement of the play. Other references take on significance when viewed in retrospect. Thus a passing remark by the departing Marquis provides us with a guide to the probable amount of time which elapses before his return: 'ce sera l'affaire d'une semaine' (I, 3, 296). Nevertheless, despite such indications, it proves difficult to be certain about the play's internal chronology. Critics are not agreed on how to interpret the evidence and Musset, it must be said, is not always clear or consistent. The best succinct analysis of the time sequence is undoubtedly that proposed by Masson. This deserves to be reproduced in full:

ACTE I — Du jeudi minuit au vendredi à la tombée de la
      nuit.
ACTE II — Du vendredi à l'heure du dîner au vendredi
      tard dans la soirée.
ACTE III — La journée du samedi.
ACTE IV — La journée du dimanche.
ACTE V — Les lundi et mardi à Florence, et, audacieuse-
      ment intercalées, deux scènes situées à Venise et qui

> se passent un peu plus tard, sans doute les mercredi
> et jeudi. (*31*, p.142)

We would, however, be unwise to look for a clear progression from scene to scene. Masson appositely remarks that there is no causal link between the separation of the Marquis from his family (I, 3) and the fainting of Lorenzo (I, 4). Were it not for the presence of the Cardinal in both scenes we might conclude that the two sets of events were taking place simultaneously. We are left with the impression that Musset is less concerned with establishing a rigorous and easily recognizable internal chronology than with achieving a general compression of real time into represented theatrical time. Events which occurred over a period of years — Nasi's ball, Louise's death, Alexandre's assassination, Lorenzo's murder — now take place within a number of days.

W.D. Howarth writes that the conventional unity of place goes by the board in Musset's play but he adds that 'the diversity of successive locations in and around Florence has the cumulative effect of creating, from the multiple aspects of the life of the city that are evoked by the playwright, a different sort of unity' (*3*, p.297). This unity is really Florence as both a physical and a moral presence. Even the scenes set in Venice do not distract attention away from the question of how to inaugurate a new condition of life in Florence. This is why the decision to set the final scene in the main square of the Tuscan capital is so successful; the population comes together in a particular space which evokes the city's past and traditions in order to participate in an act of celebration which is really a gesture of submission and humiliation.

Musset needs the multiplicity of locations both in order to make the action progress and in order to convey a full portrait of the city's life. This lends to the drama an epic quality whilst increasing its power as spectacle. The street scenes are justly famous. Here Musset succeeds in combining action and exposition. Let us take as our example the scene at Montolivet (I, 5). The first point to be noted is the number of actors on stage: '*La foule sort de l'église*'. Next we register the contrast between the flippant superficiality of the ladies of the court and the patriotic emotion of the Goldsmith. But the influence of the decor now begins to be felt. The spectator's ear hears the words of patriotism but he sees the merchants engaged in plying their trade. The interplay of sight and sound generates irony and encourages the audience's awareness of the bonds which bind the merchants to the economic and political order. Next Musset reminds us of the reality of oppression and the presence of sexuality. A noble lady shows interest in the Silk Merchant's wares. 'Montrez-moi des bas de soie' she requests and at that moment a German officer comments: 'Il n'y en aura pas d'assez petits pour vous' (I, 5, 601-02). While these actions are portrayed before us, information necessary to the exposition is being given: the towering presence of the citadel, the exiles, the difficulty of resistance — 'Quelques pauvres jeunes gens ont été tués sur le Vieux-Marché' (I, 5, 574-75) — the background to the present situation (the conduct of the Pope and the Holy Roman Emperor). Other themes emerge naturally from the conversation. The Goldsmith raises the question of artistic independence and responsibility, a matter already alluded to by Alexandre and destined to be taken up later by Tebaldeo: 'Les grands artistes n'ont pas de patrie' (I, 5, 563-64). Significantly this remark is developed in a manner which extends our vision and provides local colour: 'A propos d'artiste, ne voyez-vous pas dans ce petit cabaret ce grand gaillard qui gesticule devant des badauds? ... si je ne me trompe, c'est ce hâbleur de Cellini' (I, 5, 565-67). This short scene therefore brings together characters from different social areas (merchants, bourgeois, ladies of the court, the opposition, an officer, a 'cavalier') and reveals their divergent attitudes to Florence's predicament. In the last third of the scene Musset skilfully and unobtrusively leads us back to the plot by presenting the provocation of Léon Strozzi by Salviati.

Lorenzaccio comprises an interesting blend of interior and exterior settings. Among the interior settings we have: the Duke's Palace, the Soderini Palace, Lorenzo's bedchamber, an inn, the Strozzi Palace. But even within these settings there is a further diversity. Bernard Masson reminds us that we know at least three rooms in Ricciarda's house: a large room, a bedroom, a boudoir (*31*, p.123). Similarly if we turn to the Strozzi Palace we are shown Philippe both in his private room (suffering in isolation from personal anguish) and in a much larger room (addressing the assembled members of his clan). Musset moves easily from interior to exterior and this is a useful device which retains the audience's interest while giving an impression of the diverse nature of social life in Florence. Moreover, the technique extends our sense of space by having characters refer to events taking place off-stage but supposedly within sight of the participants. The reference to Cellini is a case in point. Another would be Giomo's remarks as Lorenzo disposes of the chain-mail shirt in the well. This blend of interior and exterior settings has a further advantage: it suggests the relationship between the private and public dimensions of human experience. The decor is not a mere backcloth; it functions in accordance with Musset's imaginative vision. Often the setting is chosen for its appropriateness. The natural scenery of the banks of the Arno corresponds to the psychology of Marie and Catherine; Tebaldeo, the believer in art's sacred mission, is first encountered on the steps of a church. The streets are so many public spaces which allow movement, exchange, commerce. But at the same time they are the location of oppression, conflict and death.

We may now turn to a short discussion of Musset's verbal style and use of dialogue. Which linguistic levels, which registers are employed in this prose drama? What effects are achieved? Robert Horville makes an interesting initial point when he observes that the characters express themselves 'dans un style identique somptueux et sensible qui est celui de Musset' (*26*, p.47). Among his examples the critic cites the Duke's remark: 'ils m'ont mis dans la main une espèce de sceptre qui sent la hache d'une lieue' (I, 4, 393-94) and the Goldsmith's comment: 'comme l'édifice branlait au vent ..., on a remplacé le pilier devenu clocher par un gros pâté informe fait de boue et de crachat' (I, 2, 181-84). The reader or spectator rapidly recognises in expressions such as these a tonality which seems typical of the playwright himself. But this strongly imaginative style is by no means employed uniformly thoughout the play. Musset is careful to endow his characters with individuality and he uses habits of speech to reveal personality. Thus Alexandre is marked by his unrefined language: 'Quant à la Cibo, j'en ai par-dessus les oreilles; hier encore, il a fallu l'avoir sur le dos pendant toute la chasse' (IV, 1, 2636-37). The Goldsmith's fondness for patriotic declarations has already been seen. Tebaldeo strikes the right note of aesthetic religiosity. Giomo's language is suited to his brutish nature: 'Ta sœur est dénichée, brave canaille' (I, 1, 60). Among the more important characters a greater linguistic variety is naturally in evidence. Ricciarda, for example, is capable of expressing tenderness, passion, patriotism, anger and self-doubt.

Musset uses dialogue in different ways. It can suggest the relationship between characters. The exchanges between Lorenzo and Alexandre point to their intimacy; the con-versations between Marie and Catherine are revelatory of the elder woman's need for emotional support. In other circum-stances dialogue testifies directly to the power of language. Lorenzo's verbal provocations and the Cardinal's treatment of his sister-in-law are obvious examples. Elsewhere dialogue conveys information concerning character: we understand Philippe's hesitations and oscillations better in the light of his conversations with his sons. Dialogue can also be used for comic effect — the contrast between the wordy phrases of the two tutors and the aggressive behaviour of their unruly charges produces a memorable moment of near farce.

The dramatist's willingness to make use of colloquialisms, unrefined language and popular speech lends to his play, and in particular to the street scenes, an air of veracity. There is, however, an obvious contrast between Musset's desire to use dialogue in this manner and his equally evident fondness for the monologue. Ricciarda, Philippe and the Cardinal as well as Lorenzo are all given the opportunity to reflect at length on their predicament in a series of monologues. In these, Musset's taste for imaginative, poetic prose is given wider reign. Act Four contains three soliloquies by Lorenzo which are essential for our understanding of his deeper motivations (IV, 3, 5, 9). They build upon the revelations given in the course of the long dialogue with Philippe in Act Three. The most significant soliloquy constitutes the ninth scene. Here Lorenzo tries to prepare himself mentally and emotionally for the murder. But he is no Cornelian hero debating with himself which course of action to follow. We are not presented with a reasoned argument. Instead the protagonist's emotional instability is powerfully rendered. His mind darts from one concern to another; from the details of the murder setting ('j'emporterai la lumière') to his mother's fate ('Que ma mère mourût de tout cela, voilà ce qui pourrait arriver'), from an apostrophe to the moon to a condemnation of the weakness of the republicans, from an imaginary verbal exchange with Alexandre to a memory of childhood at Cafaggiuolo, from a sense of fatigue ('je tombe de lassitude') to a need for frenzied activity ('j'ai des envies de danser qui sont incroyables'). In constructing a soliloquy along these lines Musset was clearly drawing inspiration from Shakespearian tragedy. W.D. Howarth remarks that whilst the classical soliloquy has as its purpose 'moral justification by logical persuasion' in Musset's hands it becomes an appeal for sympathetic understanding 'from a character conscious of having reached an extreme limit of human experience' (*3*, p.303).

Many readers continue to find the dramatic form of *Lorenzaccio* somewhat perplexing. The play inevitably challenges the expectations of the reader or spectator. The irregular plot development, the changes from dialogue to monologue, the occasionally surprising blend of colloquialism and poetic prose, all have disturbed readers and in some instances caused dissatisfaction. But it must be stressed that to search for the beauty of classical drama in Musset's creation is a fruitless task. Musset seeks a different kind of beauty, a different kind of truth. Even the superficial similarities with traditional drama turn out to be deceptive. Does the division into five acts really correspond to a dramatic progression? Hassan El Nouty notes that to introduce a substantial interlude between Acts Three and Four is to lose the effectiveness of the telling contrast between Philippe's desolation at the death of his daughter and

Alexandre's very different reaction as expressed in the opening lines of Act Four (*24*, p.598). It is also interesting to note that Musset's scenes are no more self-contained units than his acts. The printed text of Act One comprises six scenes and yet, as Howarth and El Nouty remind us, the number would immediately rise to at least sixteen had Musset followed the practice of classical tragedy and considered each entry or exit by a character as indicating a change of scene (see *3*, p.297; *24*, p.596). It is in fact much wiser to view the play as a sequence of tableaux than to endeavour to evaluate its success in respect of traditionally accepted criteria. Sices correctly observes that Musset's concept of structure 'foreshadows the Symbolist aesthetic, which values obscurity in obtaining the reader's active participation in the work of art' (*17*, p.143). Discontinuity and difficulty become necessary features of the drama. In these circumstances to look for unity exclusively in terms of time, place or action is to ignore the fact that the references to the mask, to sexuality, to language, echo through the text and construct an underlying pattern of thematic coherence. Most of all Musset has found a dramatic form which conveys his central concern: the meaninglessness of change in a world in which the interlinking of individual and collective experience only adds to human isolation and fragmentation.

Concluding Remarks

In the course of the century and a half which has elapsed since its composition, *Lorenzaccio* has lost nothing of its power to disturb. On the contrary, the modern temper responds immediately and sympathetically to the work's arresting complexity, to its refusal to explain human motivation by way of clear statement. The strength of the play lies to a large measure in its capacity to weave morality and history, individual and society, into one tissue. Musset's desire to distil the essence of Renaissance Florence does not conflict with his portrayal of the dilemma of the protagonist. Furthermore, his chosen dramatic form contributes significantly to the realisation of this overall design. *Lorenzaccio* cannot fail to disconcert, to unsettle the reader. The profound bleakness of Musset's moral vision is apparent to all. History shapes our destiny but seems cruelly indifferent to our aspirations. Action cannot transform society but neither can art redeem reality. Isolated, alienated, men remain bound to their illusions. To experience *Lorenzaccio* as a reader or as a spectator is to question the notion of the self as a fixed entity, to doubt the capacity of the personality to serve as a bulwark against the flow of time. Musset teaches us that our aims and projects may be the clothing of less avowable desires, that language does not aid the process of definition, that belief, though necessary, may be impossible.

Select Bibliography

The books and articles listed below have been chosen to help the student come to grips with modern readings of *Lorenzaccio*. A full bibliography is included in Masson's *Musset et le théâtre intérieur (31)*.

A. EDITIONS OF 'LORENZACCIO'

In the present study references are to *Lorenzaccio*, ed. D.-P. and P. Cogny (Paris, Bordas, 1963). The play is also available in the main French paperback collections: Folio, Garnier-Flammarion, Larousse. The standard critical edition is that prepared by Paul Dimoff under the title *La Genèse de Lorenzaccio* (Paris, Didier, 1964). In recent years a prestigious and expensive edition has been published: *Lorenzaccio*, ed. B. Masson (Paris, Imprimerie Nationale, 1978). The play has been published in the United Kingdom by London University Press and also by Manchester University Press.

B. GENERAL AND BACKGROUND STUDIES

1 Bowman, Frank Paul, 'Notes Towards the Definition of the Romantic Theater', *L'Esprit Créateur* (Fall 1965), 121-30.
2 El Nouty, Hassan, *Théâtre et pré-cinéma* (Paris, Nizet, 1978).
3 Howarth, W.D., *Sublime and Grotesque. A Study of French Romantic Drama* (London, Harrap, 1975).
4 Milner, Max, *Le Romantisme I 1820-1843* (Paris, Arthaud, 1973). This is volume 12 of the series *Littérature française* published under the direction of Claude Pichois.

C. CRITICAL STUDIES OF MUSSET AND HIS THEATRE

5 Affron, Charles, *A Stage for Poets: Studies in the Theatre of Hugo and Musset* (Princeton, Princeton University Press, 1971). See Chap. 9 for a discussion of *Lorenzaccio*
6 Duchet, Claude, 'Alfred de Musset', in *Histoire littéraire de la France* (Paris, Editions Sociales, 1973), vol. IV, part 2, 78-98.
7 ——, 'Un poète dans la société: Alfred de Musset', *Revue des travaux de l'Académie des sciences morales et politiques* (1969), 95-105.
8 *Europe* (Nov.-Déc. 1977). Special number devoted to Musset.
9 Gans, Eric, *Musset et le 'drame tragique'* (Paris, Corti, 1974).
10 Gochberg, Herbert, *Stage of dreams. The Dramatic Art of Alfred de Musset (1828-1834)* (Geneva, Droz, 1967).

11 Journée d'études sur Alfred de Musset (Clermont-Ferrand, Société des études romantiques, 1978). Collection of papers by various authors.

12 Lafoscade, Léon, *Le Théâtre d'Alfred de Musset* (Paris, Hachette, 1901). Reprinted by Nizet in 1966.

13 Lebois, A., *Vues sur le théâtre de Musset* (Avignon, Aubanel, 1966).

14 Lefebvre, Henri, *Alfred de Musset dramaturge* (Paris, L'Arche, 1955).

15 Pommier, Jean, *Autour du drame de Venise* (Paris, Nizet, 1958).

16 ——, *Variétés sur Alfred de Musset et son théâtre* (Paris, Nizet, 1966).

17 Sices, David, *Theater of Solitude. The Drama of Alfred de Musset* (Hanover, University Press of New England, 1974).

18 Van Tieghem, Philippe, *Musset*, nouvelle édition (Paris, Hatier, 1969).

D. CRITICAL STUDIES OF 'LORENZACCIO'

19 Bem, Jeanne, '*Lorenzaccio* entre l'Histoire et le fantasme', *Poétique* (1980), 451-61.

20 Bromfield, Joyce, *De Lorenzino de Médicis à 'Lorenzaccio'* (Paris, Didier, 1972).

21 Diaz, José, 'Le Corps et le signe. Hypothèses sémiotiques pour *Lorenzaccio* et *Les Caprices de Marianne*', *Littérature* (Oct. 1978), 43-63.

22 Duchet, Claude, 'Musset et la politique', *Revue des sciences humaines* (1962), 514-49.

23 ——, 'Théâtre et sociocritique: la crise de la parole dans deux pièces de Musset', in *Sociocritique* (Paris, Nathan, 1980), 147-56.

24 El Nouty, Hassan, 'L'Esthétique de *Lorenzaccio*', *Revue des sciences humaines* (1962), 589-611.

25 Grimsley, Ronald, 'The Character of Lorenzaccio', *French Studies* (1957), 16-27.

26 Horville, Robert, *Lorenzaccio* (Paris, Hatier, 1972).

27 Hunt, Herbert, 'Alfred de Musset et la révolution de juillet', *Mercure de France* (April 1934), 70-88.

28 Kittang, Atle, 'Action et langage dans *Lorenzaccio* d'Alfred de Musset' *Revue romane* (1975), 33-49.

29 Maclean, Marie, 'The Sword and the Flower: the Sexual Symbolism of *Lorenzaccio*', *Australian Journal of French Studies* (1979), 166-81.

30 Masson, Bernard, *Lorenzaccio ou la difficulté d'être* (Paris, Minard, 1962).

31 ——, *Musset et le théâtre intérieur* (Paris, Colin, 1974).

32 Merlant, J.-C., *Le Moment de 'Lorenzaccio' dans le destin de Musset* (Athens, Institut Français d'Athènes, 1955).

33 Moser, Walter, '*Lorenzaccio*: le carnaval et le cardinal', *Romantisme*, 19 (1978), 94-108.

34 Piemme, Jean-Marie, '*Lorenzaccio*: impasse d'une idéologie', *Romantisme*, 1-2 (1971), 117-27.

35 Ubersfeld, Anne, 'Révolution et topique de la cité: *Lorenzaccio*', *Littérature* (Déc. 1976), 40-50.

CRITICAL GUIDES TO FRENCH TEXTS

edited by

Roger Little, Wolfgang van Emden, David Williams